Anja Angelica Chan, JD

Women and Sexual Harassment: A Practical Guide to the Legal Protections of Title VII and the Hostile Environment Claim

NOTES FOR PROFESSIONAL LIBRARIANS AND LIBRARY USERS

This is an original book title published by Harrington Park Press, an imprint of The Haworth Press, Inc. Unless otherwise noted in specific chapters with attribution, materials in this book have not been previously published elsewhere in any format or language.

CONSERVATION AND PRESERVATION NOTES

The paper used in this publication meets the minimum requirements of American National Standard for Information Sciences–Permanence of Paper for Printed Material, ANSI Z39.48-1984.

Women and Sexual Harassment

A Practical Guide to the Legal Protections of Title VII and the Hostile Environment Claim

Women and Sexual Harassment

A Practical Guide to the Legal Protections of Title VII and the Hostile Environment Claim

Anja Angelica Chan, JD

Harrington Park Press
An Imprint of The Haworth Press, Inc.
New York • London • Norwood (Australia)

Published by

Harrington Park Press, an imprint of The Haworth Press, Inc., 10 Alice Street, Binghamton, NY 13904-1580

Library of Congress Cataloging-in-Publication Data

Chan, Anja Angelica.
    Women and sexual harassment : a practical guide to the legal protections of Title VII and the hostile environment claim / Anja Angelica Chan.
        p.   cm
    Includes bibliographical references and index.
    ISBN 1-56023-040-1 (acid-free paper).
    1. Sexual harassment of women–Law and legislation–United States. 2. Discrimination in employment–Law and legislation–United States. I. Title.
KF3467.C47   1993
344.73'014133–dc20
[347.30414133]   92-44322
                                                                                    CIP

ABOUT THE AUTHOR

Anja Angelica Chan, JD, is a recent graduate of Boalt, the University of California at Berkeley School of Law, where she specialized in the area of civil rights, focusing on women's issues. She became interested in the area of sexual harassment law while working as a law clerk in the labor department of Pacific Bell. Ms. Chan is a member of the California Bar Association, International Social Science Honor Society and Sociology Academic Society. Her interests include protecting the rights of both women and minorities.

CONTENTS

Preface

> To a certain extent, women have "won." In medicine, law and management, they have increased their participation by 300% to 400% since the early '70's, and no one can argue that they haven't made *some* difference. . . . But, I'm sorry, sisters, this is not the revolution. What's striking, from an old-fashioned (ca. 1970) feminist perspective, is just how *little* has changed.
>
> Ehrenreich, *Sorry, Sisters, This Is Not the Revolution,* Time Special Issue: Women The Road Ahead, Fall 1990 At 15.

To say that women have won the feminist revolution because of their increased participation in higher realms of the workforce would be to deny the experiences of most working women. Today, women continue to face a myriad of obstacles in the labor market which deny them the opportunity to participate equally. Sexual harassment is one of these obstacles. Studies indicate that many working women experience some sort of unwelcome sexual conduct on the job.[1] Sexual harassment of women is not just a bothersome annoyance, but an intolerable dynamic which operates to perpetuate women's subordinate socio-economic status.

A woman who is sexually harassed at work is likely to feel objectified, powerless, and angry. Adding to the psychological and/or physical injury caused by the initial instances of harassment is the woman's inability to remedy her situation. Most women cannot risk losing their jobs and thus do not have the luxury of resisting their harassers. Others endure harassment because their experience in the labor market has taught them that they will not be able to escape harassment by changing jobs. Those who consider complaining about harassment internally are often discouraged by the likelihood that management will not take their complaints seriously.

On the other hand, those who look to the legal system for vindication of their rights are often discouraged from filing a complaint because of prejudices in the legal system. Before November 1991 federal law failed to provide sexually harassed plaintiffs with an adequate legal remedy, further discouraging victims from bringing a claim.

Eventually, even women who are not psychologically or physically injured by unwelcome sexual advances at work are likely to feel the effects of sexual harassment because such behavior perpetuates negative stereotypes of women and secures their position as second-class citizens. For example, women who are not injured by harassment in the workplace may not be fortunate enough to escape victimization in the form of spousal abuse,[2] rape, or some other sex-based evil. These crimes are part of the same dynamic that objectifies and subordinates women in the employment context.

In addition, sexual harassment of women hurts employees of both sexes who share the victim's working environment. Deserving men and women may be passed up for promotions which are instead awarded to the objects of their supervisor's sexual desire. When an office or other work environment becomes permeated with harassment and hostility it no longer provides a productive atmosphere for any employees, regardless of their gender.

It follows from the foregoing observations that women undoubtedly have not won their revolution as long as sexual harassment prevails in the workplace. While it will be necessary to outline a comprehensive strategy to rid the workplace of harassment, that is not my objective here. Instead, I hope that this guidebook will be a valuable resource for those who use existing legal tools to fight sexual harassment in the courts. The legal tool I have chosen for the focus of this guide is the *hostile environment* sexual harassment claim.

The hostile environment claim alleges that sexual harassment has become so pervasive in a work environment that it negatively affects the employee's work performance or her psychological well-being, thus becoming a term or condition of work and a violation of Title VII of the Civil Rights Act of 1964.[3] Since there are many legal issues regarding the hostile environment claim that have yet to be decided, advocates have the opportunity–and the responsibility–

to shape the claim into a weapon that will be equitable to employers, yet effective in putting a stop to sexual harassment at work.

The content of this guide is limited in several ways. First, I recognize that sexual harassment claims exist in other spheres such as education and housing, but have chosen to focus solely on the employment setting. While discrimination against women in other spheres certainly contributes to their powerlessness, the type of economic control male supervisors exercise over their female employees makes sexual harassment of women in the workplace a particularly coercive experience that must be prevented.

Second, I have chosen to focus on hostile environment claims brought by women against men. Past discrimination against women in employment decisions has created a workplace structure in which men generally supervise women. Since, in the majority of instances, men are the ones with the power to harass, it is not surprising that women are primarily the victims and men the perpetrators of sexual harassment at work. This is not to deny that men are often victims of harassment by their female or gay male supervisors. I do not mean to imply that these other relationships do not exist, but simply choose to focus on the norm.

Third, while many states have adopted civil rights statutes similar to Title VII, as well as other remedies for sexual harassment in the workplace, this guide focuses on the federal Title VII claim. Since many state civil rights statutes are modeled after Title VII, and state courts often look to federal case law for guidance, understanding the Title VII claim is necessary in any event. Resources which describe alternative remedies, however, are also cited.

Fourth, while some references included in this guide address the harassment of minority women at work, racial harassment is not the focus. Harassment of non-minority women, and harassment of minority women, are not the same phenomenon. Because of the nature of the existing claims, courts have tried to characterize harassment as either based on race *or* on sex.[4] The issue of harassment where race and gender intersect deserves separate and special attention. I hope that this book will be useful for those who attempt to define and remedy that experience.

Practitioners wishing to educate themselves on the hostile environment claim, women who are the victims of harassment at work, and employers who are developing policies to comply with Title VII are all likely to find this guidebook useful in their research. I am particularly hopeful that it will be employed by lawyers and scholars who are interested in the state of the law for the purpose of suggesting change.

In putting together this guide I have found many unanswered questions that deserve attention, for example: "Does the reasonable person standard employed by most courts in evaluating hostile environment claims produce fair results?" "Are there alternative legal frameworks to address sexual harassment that would be more successful than Title VII?" "Could this problem be dealt with more effectively outside the legal system?" Thinking about answers to such questions is fundamentally important because as long as women in America do not have an equal voice in the marketplace, many will be forced to accept the status quo in exchange for their next paycheck. Barbara Ehrenreich's observation that little has changed is actually not so surprising when you consider how difficult it is, economically, for many women just to survive.

NOTES

1. *See,* Safran, *What Men Do to Women on the Job: A Shocking Look at Sexual Harassment,* REDBOOK 149, 217-223 (November, 1976); *U.S. Merit Systems Protection Board, Sexual Harassment in the Federal Workplace: Is It a Problem?* U.S. Government Printing Office (1981); Working Women's Institute, *Sexual Harassment on the Job–Results of Preliminary Survey,* Research Series Rep. No. 1 (1975); *U.S. Merit Systems Protection Board, Sexual Harassment in the Federal Workplace: An Update,* Report of the U.S. Merit Systems Protection Board, U.S. Government Printing Office (1988); Courie, *Women in the Large Law Firms: A High Price of Admission?* Nat. L. J. (December 11, 1989).

2. Catharine MacKinnon tells the story of a woman purchasing clerk who showed up at work with black and blue bruises after receiving a raise. Her husband had beaten her because he thought her raise must have been a result of her "putting out" for her boss. C. MACKINNON, SEXUAL HARASSMENT OF WORKING WOMEN, A CASE OF SEX DISCRIMINATION 49 (Yale Univ. Press, 1979).

3. 42 U.S.C.§2000e *et seq.*

4. *But see,* Hicks v. Gates Rubber Co., 928 F.2d 966, 970 (10th Cir. 1991) (Racial and sexual harassment must be considered in combination to determine whether harassment was sufficiently pervasive in black female employee's work environment.)

I. How to Use this Guide

As the body of sexual harassment law continues to grow at rapid speed, research is becoming increasingly difficult, even for experts in the field. For non-lawyers unaccustomed to the process of legal research, it can be particularly frustrating. This guide is designed to enable researchers interested in any aspect of the hostile environment claim to access relevant and up-to-date information in a way that saves time and prevents frustration. In light of this objective, I have organized this book so that it need not be read cover to cover. Instead, researchers should use the table of contents as well as the descriptions below to direct them to parts of the book that are appropriate for their purposes.

Part II summarizes the law relevant to the hostile environment claim. This summary covers the historical development of the claim, elements of the prima facie case, employer liability for employee acts, filing requirements, remedies, evidence, and alternative claims. Those looking to familiarize themselves with the claim should start here.

Part III is a guide to finding resources relevant to hostile environment sexual harassment and related issues. Included in the research guide are suggestions for using on-line and looseleaf services, paper indexes, special libraries and organizations to locate primary and secondary sources of information on the claim. The hostile environment claim is not well-established legal doctrine. To the contrary, it is a relatively new and rapidly developing area of law. The Supreme Court's decision in *Meritor Savings Bank v. Vinson*, [1] for example, left the question of employer liability and other crucial issues open to debate. The court's failure to resolve these issues makes it necessary to analyze current decisions to determine what standards have been adopted by the Equal Employment Opportunity Commission and by the circuits. It is also helpful to study the latest academic reviews to see which standards are suggested. In addition, constant updating is a necessity. By providing a research guide, I hope to lessen the burden of keeping up with new information on this topic.

Part IV of this guidebook lists primary sources of information on the hostile environment claim including federal court cases, agency decisions, statutes, and regulations. The pertinence of each decision is captured in an accompanying blurb. While I have not listed every hostile environment case ever heard, I have included the landmark decisions as well as many others.

References to a variety of secondary resources that I find most valuable on the topic of hostile environment sexual harassment are listed in Part V. Included are references to books, text books, treatises, surveys, briefs, policy memoranda, legislative history, annotations, encyclopedias, videos, and practitioner tools, as well as newspaper, journal, and law review articles. Though only sources that deserve attention are cited, each is evaluated for the nature and comparative value of its content.

NOTE

1. 477 U.S. 57 (1986).

II. The Claim

A. THE HISTORY

In the 1970s a series of studies made public a problem that women have been painfully aware of since they entered the labor market–the problem of sexual harassment at work. *Redbook's* 1976 reader survey and the federal government's 1980 employee study were among the most publicized. While the results of these surveys were shocking to some, to many working women the results simply confirmed their own experiences. Of the 9,000 readers who responded to *Redbook* magazine's questionnaire, 88% maintained that they had personally been harassed, while more than 90% verified that sexual harassment was a problem in their work environments.[1] The government's study of its employees revealed that over 40% had experienced sexual harassment at work in the past two years.[2]

Around the time that these survey results were reported, women began to have some success in court. The legal argument posed by women who looked to federal courts for relief was that sexual harassment at work constitutes sex discrimination, a violation of Title VII of the Civil Rights Act of 1964. Recognition of this claim, however, was slow in coming. The court's response to this argument in the first reported sexual harassment case was typical of many that followed.[3] In this case the court dismissed the claims of Jane Corne and Geneva De Vane, who complained that they were forced to resign from their clerical positions at Bausch & Lomb because continual, unsolicited, sexual advances from their male supervisor made their jobs unbearable. The court held that no discrimination had occurred since the advances complained of were unrelated to work and merely represented their supervisor's attempt to satisfy his personal urges.[4]

It was not until 1976 in *Williams v. Saxbe*[5] that a federal court held that sexual advances made by a male supervisor to his female employee constitutes sex discrimination actionable under Title VII. Unlike previous courts, the court in *Williams* focused primarily on whether or not Williams had suffered retaliation from refusing her supervisor's advances *based upon her sex*. In a landmark decision, Judge Richey held that "the conduct of the plaintiff's supervisor created an artificial barrier to employment which was placed before one gender and not the other, despite the fact that both genders are similarly situated."[6] Such discrimination based on sex, he held, violated Title VII. A year later in *Barnes v. Costle*,[7] the D.C. Circuit also found that a male supervisor who retaliated against a female employee for refusing his sexual propositions violated Title VII. This time, however, the broad language of the court apparently extended Title VII's protection to women who are victims of harassment based on sex but who have not yet experienced retaliation.[8]

By the late 1970s the federal courts had taken a big step forward, giving a legal definition to the unwanted sexual behavior that working women across the nation were forced to endure. Recognizing that such behavior was based on sex, however, was not a signal that the courts fully understood the ramifications of sexual harassment. Instead, women suffering from unrelenting propositions, verbal assaults of a sexual nature, and even sexual touching were still denied relief in court if they could not demonstrate tangible job detriment. Even though feminist legal scholars like Catharine MacKinnon explained in the 1970s that sexual harassment without tangible job detriment was also a violation of Title VII, it took almost another decade before the United States Supreme Court formally recognized the hostile environment claim.

As early as 1971 federal courts recognized the idea that harassment based on race that creates a hostile or offensive work environment for minority employees violates Title VII.[9] According to the Fifth Circuit, "[T]he phrase 'terms, conditions or privileges of employment' in [Title VII] is an expansive concept which sweeps within its protective ambit the practice of creating a working environment heavily charged with ethnic or racial discrimination."[10] During the 1970s this principle was also applied to harassment based on religion and national origins.[11]

Finally, in 1981 the Court of Appeals for the D.C. Circuit applied the theory to harassment based on sex, and the hostile environment sexual harassment claim was born.[12] In *Bundy v. Jackson,* the court held that a woman who was propositioned by five of her supervisors over a two-and-a-half-year period, but was unable to show lost job benefits, stated a Title VII claim. Shortly thereafter, the Eleventh Circuit in *Henson v. City of Dundee* followed the D.C. Circuit's lead, finding that:

> Sexual harassment which creates a hostile or offensive environment for members of one sex is every bit the arbitrary barrier to sexual equality at the workplace that racial harassment is to racial equality. Surely, a requirement that a man or woman run a gauntlet of sexual abuse in return for the privilege of being allowed to work and make a living can be as demeaning and disconcerting as the harshest of racial epithets.[13]

Three years later the Supreme Court quoted this language from *Henson,* agreeing that sexual harassment based on a hostile work environment is indeed prohibited by Title VII.[14]

B. THE DEFINITION

Under Title VII of the Federal Civil Rights Act of 1964 it is unlawful for an employer to discriminate against an employee based on a person's sex. Title VII prohibits such discrimination whenever an employer makes decisions involving compensation, terms, conditions, or privileges of employment.[15] In interpreting Title VII, the Supreme Court determined that sexual harassment is a form of sex-based discrimination that is prohibited by the language of the statute. The court explained in *Meritor* that Title VII prohibits two types of sexual harassment. Both, "harassment that involves the conditioning of concrete employment benefits on sexual favors, and harassment that, while not affecting economic benefits, creates a hostile or offensive working environment,"[16] were recognized by the court. The former claim is called *quid pro quo.* This guide, however, focuses on the latter, *hostile environment* claim.

Quid pro quo harassment violates the language of Title VII because compliance with sexual behavior is made a *term* or *condition* of a woman's continued employment, promotion, or other job-related benefit. For example, Title VII is violated when a male supervisor tells a female employee that she will receive a favorable review only if she complies with his sexual requests. If she refuses to comply and then receives a poor performance review making her ineligible for promotion, tangible job detriment resulting from the quid pro quo is easy to identify. The federal courts' initial reluctance to recognize the hostile environment claim indicates that where tangible job detriment is difficult to pinpoint, the Title VII violation is also more difficult to see.

The hostile environment claim is based on the well-supported premise that women who are sexually harassed at work feel humiliated, angry, and/or frightened, often making it difficult for them to fulfill their job-related responsibilities. Since courts consider psychological well-being a *term, condition,* or *privilege* of employment, harassment which negatively affects a woman's psychological well-being alters the circumstances of her employment that are protected by statute. Where no psychological injury exists, but harassment nevertheless affects the victim's ability to perform her job, the circumstances of her employment are similarly affected. [17] Assuming that but for her gender a woman would not have been harassed, it becomes evident that hostile environment sexual harassment is sex discrimination prohibited by Title VII. This logic recognizes that women who cannot demonstrate tangible job detriment enabling them to bring a quid pro quo claim may, nevertheless, be injured by workplace harassment.

The government agency designed to enforce Title VII's provisions, the Equal Employment Opportunity Commission (EEOC), [18] also distinguishes hostile environment from quid pro quo claims. The EEOC defines hostile environment sexual harassment as follows:

> Unwelcome sexual advances, requests for sexual favors, and other verbal or physical conduct of a sexual nature constitute sexual harassment when . . . such conduct has the purpose or effect of unreasonably interfering with an individual's work

performance or creating an intimidating, hostile, or offensive working environment.[19]

Although courts are not bound to follow EEOC regulations, the Supreme Court has suggested that lower courts pay attention to the Commission's regulations and use its policy for guidance when considering sexual harassment claims.[20]

To state a Title VII sexual harassment claim under the hostile environment theory, a plaintiff must allege facts sufficient to prove that (1) she belongs to a protected class, (2) she was subjected to unwelcome sexual harassment, (3) the harassment she complains of was based on sex, (4) the harassment she complains of is sufficiently severe or pervasive so as to alter the terms and conditions of employment and create an abusive working environment, and (5) her employer is liable for the employee's unlawful conduct. These elements of the hostile environment claim are discussed in more detail below.

C. PLAINTIFF BELONGS TO A PROTECTED CLASS

As is the case with any discrimination claim brought under Title VII, plaintiffs must prove that they belong to a class of people protected by the statute. Subsection 2000e-2(a)(1) of the Civil Rights Act[21] clearly enumerates sex as a protected status. In order to fulfill this element of the hostile environment claim, therefore, a plaintiff must allege in her complaint and establish in court that she is a woman. This element is usually satisfied by stipulation.

D. HARASSMENT WAS UNWELCOME

In the words of the Supreme Court, "The gravamen of any sexual harassment claim is that the alleged sexual advances were 'unwelcome.'"[22] To bring a successful hostile environment claim, a plaintiff must demonstrate to the trier of fact that the harassing conduct alleged in the complaint was in fact unwelcome.

Though it is clear from *Meritor* that unwelcomeness is the standard, it is less clear what this standard means. Rather than defining unwelcomeness, the Supreme Court issued a vague warning that determining whether conduct is actually unwelcome "presents difficult problems of proof and turns largely on credibility determinations committed to the trier of fact."[23] On the issue of unwelcomeness the court found that evidence of Michele Vinson's compliance with her supervisor's requests for sex, while establishing voluntary submission, says nothing about whether his advances were welcomed.

Since the Supreme Court's holding only indicates what is irrelevant to the unwelcomeness inquiry, it is necessary to look to the lower courts and the EEOC to determine what facts are relevant. Years before the Supreme Court handed down its decision in *Meritor*, the Eleventh Circuit held that unwelcomeness was an essential element of the hostile environment claim. In order to demonstrate unwelcomeness, the court in *Henson* required the plaintiff to prove that: (1) she did not objectively solicit or entice the conduct in any way, and that (2) she subjectively regarded the conduct as undesirable or offensive.[24] This definition was repeated by the EEOC in the *EEOC: Policy Guidance on Sexual Harassment.*[25] After adopting *Henson's* general definition of unwelcomeness, the Commission makes several further observations regarding the unwelcomeness element of the claim.

First, along the lines of the Supreme Court's statement in *Meritor,* the Commission indicates that unwelcomeness is determined on a case-by-case basis by evaluating the totality of the circumstances and the record as a whole.[26]

Second, the Commission states that a victim's contemporaneous protest to offensive conduct will significantly strengthen a claim. When circumstances indicate that the conduct may have been welcome or when the credibility of the parties is at issue, timely protest is especially important to lend credence to the plaintiff's claim that the conduct was unwelcome.[27] If, for example, the victim had a consensual relationship with her harasser in the past, it would be difficult to prove under *Henson's* definition that she did not entice his advances unless she can demonstrate to the trier of fact that she complained about his subsequent behavior. While contemporaneous protest may be helpful to show unwelcomeness, the *Policy*

Guidance Memorandum clearly states that protest is not a necessary element of the claim.[28]

Third, the Commission derives from its analysis of agency decisions and court cases that occasional sexual banter or use of sexually explicit language by the victim at work will not necessarily foreclose a hostile environment claim. Regular instigation of sexual conversations with coworkers may, however, contradict her allegation that the harasser's conduct was unwelcome.[29] In addition, the Commission notes that by refusing to adopt the Court of Appeals finding that evidence of a victim's provocative dress and sexual fantasies is per se inadmissible, the Supreme Court in *Meritor* indicates that such evidence is also relevant to this element of the claim.[30]

From what authorities have said about the unwelcomeness issue to date there are two important things to understand: (1) voluntary compliance with sexual requests does not bar a hostile environment claim because compliance can be voluntary even when the behavior is unwelcome; and (2) when welcomeness is at issue the trier of fact will determine whether the totality of the circumstances indicate that the victim's conduct is consistent or inconsistent with her assertion that the conduct complained of was unwelcome.

E. HARASSMENT WAS BASED ON SEX

To satisfy this element of a hostile environment claim a plaintiff must prove to the trier of fact that she was harassed *because of* her gender. This element essentially requires the plaintiff to show that she would not have been subjected to harassment, or would not have experienced the conduct as offensive, *but for* the fact that she is a woman. When unwelcome conduct would be as offensive to a man, as it is to the woman, her Title VII hostile environment claim will fail. This logic stems from the fact that Title VII was enacted to prohibit discrimination based on the protected category of sex. Title VII is successful, therefore, in preventing the most frequent form of harassment where a female employee is harassed by a heterosexual male supervisor or co-worker. Title VII, however, does not prohibit a bisexual employee from harassing others at work. For example, it would be difficult for a woman to establish that she would not have been harassed by her bisexual supervisor if she were a man when her harasser is sexually attracted to both men and women. While it probably cannot be said that male heterosexual defendants will claim bisexuality in order to avoid liability for sexual harassment charges, this loophole nevertheless demonstrates a weakness in Title VII's approach.

The but-for requirement of causation includes several categories of conduct described by the court in *Robinson v. Jacksonville Shipyards, Inc.*[32] The willingness of some federal courts to recognize many forms of behavior as based on sex reflects a growing understanding that sexual harassment has more to do with power relations than it does with uncontrollable sex drives. First, courts have clearly stated that harassment need not be sexually suggestive for it to be considered based on sex. According to the court in Robinson, "harassing behavior lacking a sexually explicit content but directed at women and motivated by animus against women satisfies this [but-for] requirement.[33] For example, comments from a supervisor like "women just aren't cut out for this work," "you belong at home," or "you bitches are all alike" will be considered along with sexually suggestive behavior when determining the severity and pervasiveness of hostility in the work environment. In *Robinson,* the court held that a "Men Only" sign painted on the door of an employee trailer illustrates this form of harassment.[34]

Second, courts recognize that sexually suggestive conduct is based on sex. Come-ons, comments that refer to sex or to a woman's body, and sexually provocative touching are among the easiest forms of conduct to define as sexual harassment. Courts have held that such conduct directed at women raises the inference that the harassment is based on sex.[35]

Third, several federal courts have acknowledged that conduct that is not directed at an individual or group of individuals, but is disproportionately more offensive or demeaning to one sex is also actionable.[36] According to the court in *Robinson:*

> This third category describes behavior that creates a barrier to
> the progress of women in the workplace because it conveys
> the message that they do not belong, that they are welcome in
> the workplace only if they will subvert their identities to the

sexual stereotypes prevalent in that environment. That Title VII outlaws such conduct is beyond peradventure.[37]

A common form of conduct which falls under this category is the hanging of pornographic pin-ups in the work environment. Even where offense is not intended, the presence of pin-ups in the workplace has a disproportionately demeaning impact on women because it sends the message that women do not belong.

Characterization of the conduct complained of in accordance with the categories described above may help a plaintiff demonstrate to the court how Title VII was violated. Plaintiffs should never assume that the sex-based nature of the conduct is self-evident.

F. HARASSMENT WAS SUFFICIENTLY SEVERE OR PERVASIVE

Under current law, a plaintiff bringing a hostile environment claim must demonstrate that the conduct complained of was sufficiently severe or pervasive so as to alter the conditions of employment and create a hostile or abusive working environment. In many cases plaintiffs fail to meet this burden.

There are two main issues to address in regard to this element of the claim. First, it is necessary to determine which standard will be used by the trier of fact to judge whether the sufficiently severe or pervasive requirement has been met. Second, it is helpful to be familiar with the kind of evidence a trier of fact will consider in determining whether the element has been met.

One of the main uncertainties regarding the hostile environment claim is the standard that will be used to judge whether the conduct complained of was sufficiently severe or pervasive. To meet this element of the prima facie case, some circuits require plaintiffs to demonstrate that the harassment was so severe it would have interfered with the work performance or the psychological well-being of a *reasonable person* in similar circumstances.[38] Others ask the trier of fact to determine whether a *reasonable woman* would consider the conduct complained of so severe that it would have interfered with work performance or psychological well-being.[39]

The reasonable woman standard does not create more protection for women than for men under Title VII, but simply acknowledges the bias inherent in the reasonable person standard. In his dissenting opinion in *Rabidue v. Osceola Refining Co.,* Judge Keith explains that the reasonable person standard allows courts to evaluate the conduct complained of by comparing it to ingrained notions of reasonable behavior that have been fashioned by male offenders.[40] Using outmoded but deeply ingrained definitions of appropriate gender behavior as the yardstick for acceptable conduct will permit rather than prohibit men from harassing women at work. To accomplish its goal of putting women on equal footing in the workplace, Title VII must instead protect women from the injuries they suffer by adopting a standard which takes existing biases into account.

In *Ellison v. Brady,* Judge Beezer of the Ninth Circuit describes another aspect of the bias inherent in the reasonable person standard:

> Women who are victims of mild forms of sexual harassment may understandably worry whether a harasser's conduct is merely a prelude to violent sexual assault. Men, who are rarely victims of sexual assault, may view sexual conduct in a vacuum without a full appreciation of the social setting or the underlying threat of violence that a woman may perceive.[41]

The court goes on to recognize that under the reasonable woman standard adopted in *Ellison*, conduct may be characterized as harassment even when the harasser is unaware that his behavior has created a hostile environment. This effect is justified, according to the court, because Title VII does not establish a fault-based tort scheme.[42] By adopting this standard the court puts the responsibility on employers to teach their employees what type of conduct reasonable women consider sexual harassment.

Regardless of whether the court adopts a reasonable person or reasonable woman standard, two things are certain. First, no matter which standard is used, the requirement of reasonability will always protect employers from sexual harassment claims brought by hypersensitive employees.[43] Second, in addition to requiring the plaintiff to show that a hypothetical employee would be affected, courts also require the plaintiff to demonstrate that she was actually offended.[44]

Another issue to consider in regard to the reasonable person standard is which characteristics to attribute to the hypothetical person. Courts require that conduct be judged from the viewpoint of a hypothetical person in the *same or similar circumstances* as the victim.[45] How courts should decide which of the victim's circumstances to attribute to the hypothetical person, however, is not clear from the decisions. As discussed above, the trier of fact may or may not be asked to consider the victim's gender in assessing the severity of harassment. On the other hand, the trier of fact will probably be asked to evaluate the evidence as if he or she were in the same employment-related circumstances as the victim when the alleged harassment took place. If a victim complaining of harassment by physical touching had previously been raped by her boss at a former job, should the trier of fact determine whether a reasonable person *who had previously been raped at work* would find the touching sufficiently severe to affect job performance or psychological well-being?[46] The courts have not stated where to draw the line dividing circumstances of the victim that should, and those that should not, be attributed to the hypothetical person.

The second main issue to address under the sufficiently severe or pervasive element is the relevancy of various facts to the analysis. According to the courts, the question of whether the conduct complained of was so severe that it interfered with the plaintiff's work performance or psychological well-being is answered by looking at the totality of the circumstances.[47] Several factors are relevant to this analysis including: (1) the nature of the unwelcome sexual acts; (2) the frequency of the offensive encounters; (3) the total number of days over which all of the offensive conduct occurs; and (4) the context in which the sexually harassing conduct occurs.[48]

The nature of unwelcome sexual conduct is clearly relevant in establishing whether the sufficiently severe element is met. For example, courts generally find physical touching more offensive than unwelcome verbal abuse.[49] When the trier of fact is instructed to use a reasonable woman standard it is more likely that the differing nature of unwelcome verbal and physical acts will be taken into account. Even when a reasonable person standard is employed, however, the plaintiff is required to demonstrate that the alleged harassment actually affected her work performance or psychological well-being. In assessing her credibility, it is also important for the trier of fact to understand the way in which women perceive the nature of different types of conduct. A plaintiff should not presume that this understanding exists, but should carefully explain the way in which the nature of the alleged acts offended her.

For example, some may view the presence of obscene pictures in the workplace as an embarrassing factor for women to endure. Many may fail to understand, however, that such pin-ups are not just embarrassing. Instead, the presence of obscene photographs or other paraphernalia in the workplace sends messages to women that are more offensive in nature and can be sufficiently severe so as to affect work performance and psychological well-being.[50]

At one level, pictures of nude women are undoubtedly embarrassing since nudity usually occurs in private. The message may be more offensive, however, if pornography in the workplace exhibits the submission of women to men. At yet another level, the presence of obscene pin-ups reminds women that they are intruders in the workplace who do not belong. Allowing such a message to be sent without holding the sender responsible flies directly in the face of Title VII's equal opportunity ethos.

In *Rabidue* the Sixth Circuit expresses a different view:

> Indeed, it cannot seriously be disputed that in some work environments, humor and language are rough hewn and vulgar. Sexual jokes, sexual conversations and the girlie magazines may abound. Title VII was not meant to–nor can–change this. It must never be forgotten that Title VII is the federal court mainstay in the struggle for equal employment opportunity for the female workers of America. But it is quite different to claim that Title VII was designed to bring about a magical transformation in the social mores of American workers.[51]

To the contrary, Title VII mandates exactly this kind of change. Ultimately the court's decision in *Rabidue* to dismiss the plaintiff's hostile environment claim stemmed from the court's misperception of the true nature of the conduct at issue.

The factors enumerated above which facilitate an analysis of the totality of the circumstances operate on a sliding scale. The more offensive the nature of the act, the fewer times such behavior must occur, and the shorter the period over which it must occur, in order for it to create a hostile and offensive working environment. According to the courts, isolated incidents of unwelcome conduct do not create a hostile working environment. Instead, courts look for ongoing incidents or patterns of discriminatory behavior to satisfy this element of the claim.[52] In its *Policy Guidance Memorandum* the EEOC agrees that a single incident or remark will not create an abusive environment sufficient to state a claim unless the conduct is very severe.[53]

Common sense dictates that a hostile environment might be created by a supervisor who locks a female employee in his office, attempts to remove her clothes, and threatens to fire her if she does not submit to intercourse, even if this behavior is not repeated. On the other hand, a less aggressive sexual come-on or a few obscene comments about an employee's physical attributes are less likely to be sufficiently severe or pervasive so as to affect the employee's work performance or psychological well-being. If such comments become frequent and continue over a period of time, however, they may constitute a legal claim.[54]

Considering the context in which the sexually harassing conduct occurs also helps the trier of fact determine whether it was sufficiently severe or pervasive to create a hostile or abusive environment. Especially important to the analysis of context is the relationship between victim and perpetrator, as well as the relationship between the plaintiff's immediate working environment and the area where the alleged conduct occurred. Harassing conduct that occurs during a lunch date with a co-worker who works in a department far removed from the plaintiff, for example, would have a lesser impact on the woman's work performance or psychological well-being than harassing conduct which occurs when her immediate supervisor comes into her office to meet with her about a work-related matter. Harassment that occurs in the plaintiff's immediate working environment is often more offensive because she is unable to avoid the conduct and perform her job simultaneously.

Perhaps the most important factor to consider in determining whether the totality of the circumstances indicates that the harassment was sufficiently severe and pervasive to create a hostile or abusive working environment is the relationship of the victim and perpetrator. Those who disregard the relevance of this relationship mistakenly believe that sexual harassment is primarily about sex games at work. To the contrary, sexual harassment is about the power men as a group exercise over women in the labor market. If, as in *Robinson,* the victim is one of very few women employees and the perpetrators are a group of men whose acts appear to be ratified by other male co-workers, the conduct is extremely offensive. Unwelcome sexual conduct in this context sends the victim a clear message that she is an intruder in the workplace by reminding her of the historical myth that a woman's place is in the home.

Similarly, when the perpetrator is a higher-ranking male employee, unwelcome sexual conduct may be extremely offensive because it sends the message that if a woman wishes to remain in the workplace she must accept that a man's supervisory authority includes access to her sexual abilities as well as her work-related skills. It is not shocking that a single mother in an unskilled position would allow her supervisor to sexually harass her in exchange for the paycheck which enables her to feed her children. Her lack of a better alternative which results from the unequal distribution of power in the relationship is what makes the harassment particularly offensive.

A woman does not have to be an economically destitute, unskilled competitor in the labor market, however, to be forced to make such no-win decisions. For example, a young woman just out of law school who goes to work for a high-powered firm where she is harassed by a senior partner will be forced to make the no-win choice of accepting the behavior or risking her career.[55] A tenured professor subjected to the same type of behavior from a co-worker, while still a victim, is not coerced in the same way that the women in the previous examples are.

It is clear from the type of analysis that is undertaken by the trier of fact under this element of the claim that the choice between a reasonable person and a reasonable woman standard will have a significant impact on the outcome of a case. Regardless of the standard employed, however, it is the plaintiff's job to demonstrate that the conduct complained of was so severe or pervasive that it affected her work performance or psychological well-being, thus creating a hostile and offensive working environment. Only behavior of this caliber violates Title VII.

G. WOMEN WHO ARE NOT THE OBJECT OF HARASSMENT

While there has been no holding from the Supreme Court on this issue, the D.C. Circuit, in dicta, stated that a woman who is not herself the object of harassment might still have a hostile environment claim.[56] If a woman is forced to work in an atmosphere in which sexual harassment of others is severe and pervasive it may affect her ability to do her job or her psychological well-being and thus violate Title VII. If such a claim is actionable at all, courts are likely to require that the unwelcome behavior permeate the plaintiff's immediate working environment. At present, however, the law in this area remains unclear.

H. EMPLOYER LIABILITY

Title VII prohibits employers from discriminating against an individual with respect to the terms or conditions of employment on the basis of sex. According to the statute the term "employer" includes any "person engaged in an industry affecting commerce who has fifteen or more employees for each working day in each of twenty or more calendar weeks in the current or preceding calendar year."[57] The doctrine of employer liability, while crucial to a plaintiff's case, is difficult to decipher. To avoid confusion it is necessary to distinguish several factors.

First, the nature of the particular claim must be analyzed. Employer liability rules for a quid pro quo claim are different than for a hostile environment claim. Often both forms of harassment occur at once, so the possibility of overlap should be considered. Where sexual harassment has quid pro quo as well as hostile environment characteristics, it may be beneficial to allege quid pro quo harassment, since employers will be held strictly liable for a supervisor's conduct only under this type of claim.[58] For example, when creation of a hostile work environment results in constructive discharge, it can be argued that the plaintiff's continued employment was conditioned upon the quid pro quo that she endure sexual harassment without protest.[59] If the plaintiff alleged only hostile environment sexual harassment in this situation, she would bear the additional burden of proving facts sufficient to demonstrate employer liability under agency principles.

Assuming that a plaintiff brings a hostile environment claim, the second important factor to consider is the status of the perpetrator. His status as either a co-worker or supervisor will determine what set of employer liability rules apply.[60] Take first the issue of employer liability for the acts of supervisory personnel addressed in *Meritor.* Even though the court in *Meritor* ultimately decided not to issue a definitive rule on employer liability, there are five guidelines for employer liability that come from the case:

1. Employers are not automatically liable for sexual harassment by supervisory personnel.[61]
2. The absence of notice to an employer does not necessarily insulate the employer from liability.[62]
3. The mere existence of a grievance procedure and a general policy against discrimination, coupled with the plaintiff's failure to invoke procedure, is not enough to insulate the employer from liability.[63]
4. The argument that a plaintiff's failure to complain insulates the employer from liability is stronger if the employer's procedures are calculated to encourage victims of harassment to come forward.[64]
5. In enacting Title VII, Congress wanted courts to look to agency principles for guidance in the area of employer liability.[65]

These points are enumerated not because they answer the question of employer liability for supervisory acts, but because they are the only clues the Supreme Court has given as to how liability should be determined. Essentially, all the Supreme Court says in *Meritor* is that employers are not automatically liable for the acts of their supervisors, but may be held liable under agency theory. What is not clear from the Supreme Court's analysis is how agency principles should be applied. Since *Meritor,* the EEOC has provided the most guidance on the manner in which agency principles apply to the issue of employer liability in a hostile environment claim.

According to the Commission's *Policy Guidance Memorandum*, employers may be liable for acts of their supervisory personnel in one of two ways. First, the EEOC outlines the concept of direct employer liability. The Commission states that an employer will be directly liable for the acts of a supervisor that the employer had actual or constructive knowledge of if the employer fails to take immediate and appropriate corrective action.[66] An employer who acquires knowledge from first-hand observation, from the victim's complaint to other supervisors, or from the victim's charges of discrimination has *actual* knowledge.[67] An employer is deemed to have *constructive* knowledge when the employer, upon reasonably diligent inquiry, should have known of the harassment. Where harassment is pervasive in the work environment or is openly practiced, a court is likely to find that the employer had constructive knowledge of its existence.[68]

Once it is established that the employer had actual or constructive knowledge of harassment, direct liability will attach unless the employer took prompt and appropriate remedial action. In determining whether corrective action was immediate and appropriate the following responses are relevant:

1. Investigate promptly and thoroughly.[69]
2. Take steps reasonably calculated to end the harassment without adversely affecting the terms or conditions of the victim's employment.[70]
3. Compensate the victim by restoring lost employment benefits.[71]
4. Prevent the misconduct from recurring.[72]
5. Take disciplinary action against perpetrator which reflects the severity of the conduct.[73]
6. Make follow-up inquiries to ensure that harassment has not resumed and that the victim has not suffered retaliation.[74]

This is not a comprehensive list of responses necessary to escape liability, but merely points to the relevant issues. There is no clear line that divides prompt and appropriate responses from others; however, the employer must demonstrate to the trier of fact via their

response that they understand the illicit nature of sexual harassment, take it seriously, and make concerted efforts to protect their
employees from its effects.[75] Not all circuits employ this analysis.
The Seventh Circuit, for example, simply compares the employer's
response to what a reasonable employer would do to remedy harassment.[76]

The second way in which employers can be liable for the acts of
their supervisory personnel, according to the EEOC, is by imputing
liability.[77] Liability will be imputed to the employer if the plaintiff
demonstrates that the supervisor was acting within the scope of his
employment when he behaved in the manner complained of.[78] Liability will also be imputed to the employer if the plaintiff demonstrates that an exception to the scope-of-employment doctrine is
invoked.[79] Unfortunately, scope-of-employment doctrine is not
easy to apply to the issue of employer liability in a hostile environment claim.

Normally, a supervisor's acts are not within the scope of employment unless the supervisor, through his actions, exercises authority
actually vested in him by his employer. Common sense dictates that
employers will rarely authorize a supervisor to sexually harass other
employees at work. This doctrine seems to lead to the conclusion
that liability will rarely, if ever, be imputed to employers. The
EEOC, however, reaches a different result. According to the Commission, employers who have knowledge of sexual harassment perpetrated by a supervisor and do not respond with corrective action
will have liability imputed to them.[80] Presumably, an employer
grants authority to the supervisor through the employer's acquiescence to the harassment, bringing the supervisor's acts within the
scope of his employment.

Even where scope-of-employment doctrine does not allow a
plaintiff to hold her employer liable for the acts of supervisory
personnel, the EEOC describes several other theories under which
liability may be imputed. First, the EEOC explains that under the
apparent authority exception to the scope-of-employment doctrine,
employers are liable for the acts of their supervisors that third
parties reasonably believe represent expressions of authority given
to the supervisor by the employer, even when that authority was not
actually given.[81]

The Commission states that a victim could reasonably believe that the perpetrator had authority from his employer to sexually harass her if the employer had no meaningful policy against sexual harassment and no effective procedure to file complaints.[82] As explained by the Commission in its *Policy Guidance Memorandum*:

> This apparent authority of supervisors arises from their power over their employees, including the power to make or substantially influence hiring, firing, promotion and compensation decisions. A supervisor's capacity to create a hostile environment is enhanced by the degree of authority conferred on him by the employer, and he may rely upon apparent authority to force an employee to endure a harassing environment for fear of retaliation. If the employer has not provided an effective avenue to complain, then the supervisor has unchecked, final control over the victim and it is reasonable to impute his abuse of this power to the employer.[83]

According to this logic, an employer will escape liability if the employer maintains a strong policy and procedure to combat harassment in the workplace.

Agency by estoppel is another concept explained by the EEOC in its *Policy Guidance Memorandum*. Agency by estoppel also allows plaintiffs to impute liability for a supervisor's acts to his employer. Under this theory, employers are liable when they intentionally or carelessly cause an employee to mistakenly believe that the supervisor is acting on behalf of the employer. The Commission gives two examples of occasions on which an employer will be estopped from claiming that a supervisor was not acting as an agent. When a hostile environment is created by a supervisor due to the fact that the employer was negligent in supervising him, the employer will be held liable. Similarly, when an employer fails to correct prior known instances of harassment, agency by estoppel will apply.[84]

Title VII affords employees the right to work in an environment free from discriminatory intimidation, ridicule, and insult[85] The courts have placed the affirmative duty of maintaining such environments on employers' shoulders. Thus, according to the EEOC, liability may also be imputed to employers who delegate this duty to others who fail to fulfill its commands. This theory rests on the principle that employers should not be allowed to escape liability by delegating to others duties imposed by statute.[86] The court in *Brooms v. Regal Tube Co.*[87] recognized this theory when it held Regal Tube Co. liable for a hostile environment created by a manager to whom the employer had delegated the duty to prevent workplace harassment.

Finally, the EEOC's *Policy Guidance Memorandum* explains that employers are liable for harassment that is facilitated by the use of authority given to supervisors.[88] The Commission cites *Sparks v. Pilot Freight Carriers, Inc.*[89] as an example of this aiding and abetting theory. In *Sparks*, the plaintiff's supervisor used the authority given to him by his employer to threaten her with termination so that she would comply with his demands. This aiding and abetting theory would be more useful to plaintiffs if courts recognized that the fact that a supervisor has such authority is enough on its own to establish liability. Whether or not the threat of termination is spoken should be irrelevant since the message still comes across loud and clear.

The basis for the distinction between the strict liability standard in quid pro quo claims and the agency standards used in hostile environment claims rests on this notion of the illicit use of authority. In a quid pro quo claim, courts have found it easier to hold the employer strictly liable since the supervisor uses the authority granted him by his employer to condition his subordinate's employment benefits on compliance with his sexual requests. Thus, courts do not require any additional showing from the plaintiff to establish employer liability. In a hostile environment claim, however, courts do not see as clearly the connection between the employer's grant of decision-making authority to the supervisor and the supervisor's acts of sexual harassment which create a hostile working environment. Thus, courts require an additional showing from the plaintiff to establish employer liability.

Upon closer scrutiny, it should become evident that there may not be a sufficient reason for requiring hostile environment plaintiffs to bear this additional burden. Justice Marshall, concurring in *Meritor,* explains that a supervisor is not only charged with making personnel decisions that affect his subordinates, but is also charged with the "day-to-day supervision of the work environment and with ensuring a safe, productive workplace."[90] In the words of Justice Marshall:

> There is no reason why abuse of the latter authority should have different consequences than abuse of the former. In both cases it is the authority vested in the supervisor by the employer that enables him to commit the wrong: it is precisely because the supervisor is understood to be clothed with the employer's authority that he is able to impose unwelcome sexual conduct on subordinates.[91]

For this reason, states like California have elected to hold employers strictly liable for hostile environment sexual harassment perpetrated by supervisory personnel in violation of state anti-discrimination laws.[92]

There is more agreement regarding the appropriate standard to use in the determination of employer liability for the acts of non-supervisory employees in a hostile environment claim. The following standard set forth by the EEOC has been adopted by the courts:

> With respect to conduct between fellow employees, an employer is responsible for acts of sexual harassment in the workplace where the employer (or its agents or supervisory employees) knows or should have known of the conduct, unless it can show that it took immediate and appropriate actions.[93]

The meaning of the known or should have known standard and the factors relevant to the immediate and appropriate analysis are discussed above.

I. STATUTE OF LIMITATIONS

There are no substantive defenses to a hostile environment claim.[94] There are, however, certain filing requirements which the plaintiff must meet in order to bring a claim. Title VII states that a plaintiff must file charges with the EEOC within 180 days of the alleged discrimination unless the plaintiff initially institutes proceedings with a state or local agency.[95] According to Title VII, complaints must first be filed with a state or local agency that has jurisdiction over the alleged unfair employment practice.[96] Charges cannot be filed with the EEOC until 60 days after proceedings have commenced under state or local law. If the state or local proceedings are terminated before 60 days have passed, the plaintiff can file with the EEOC at that time.[97]

Usually, proceedings in a state or local agency commence with the filing of a written statement of facts upon which the charge is based. Regardless of when they actually commence, however, state or local proceedings will be deemed to begin when the statement is sent by registered mail to the state or local authority.[98] Note that this requirement does not necessitate exhaustion of state or local remedies before filing with the EEOC, but merely creates a 60-day waiting period. In the year after a state or local law has been enacted, this 60-day waiting period is extended to 120 days.[99] Should a complainant file with the EEOC when charges properly should have been brought to the state or local agency first, the EEOC will transmit the charge to the appropriate agency and no rights will be lost.[100]

A complainant may file directly with the EEOC when no state or local agency has been authorized to grant relief or when the relief it is authorized to grant is inadequate.[101] Where the complainant is required to file first with a state or local agency, the period in which she must file with the EEOC is extended from 180 days to 300 days from the time the alleged unlawful employment practice occurred, or to within 30 days after the state or local agency has notified her of the termination of its proceedings, whichever is earlier.[102]

Federal courts have held that the limitation period does not begin to run until after the pattern of discrimination has ended. This doctrine of continuing violations enables plaintiffs to recover for acts that predate the limitations period when those acts are part of an ongoing pattern. In *Chung v. Romona Valley Community Hospital*,[103] the court held that a plaintiff claiming discrimination under Title VII could recover for acts predating the limitations period even when his EEOC charge did not allege a pattern of acts under this theory. It was enough, according to the court, that his EEOC charge alleged a number of acts that suggested such a pattern. It is advisable, however, that plaintiffs filing hostile environment charges with the EEOC or state or local agencies set out the ongoing nature of the harassment in their statement of facts to enable the investigator to consider all the acts when judging the pervasiveness and severity of abuse in the environment.

J. REMEDIES

On November 21, 1991, Congress enacted amendments to Title VII which instituted a long-awaited change to its remedial scheme.[104] The amendments provided much-needed incentives for victims of sexual harassment at work to enforce federal anti-discrimination law through litigation. Prior to the 1991 amendment, victims of sexual harassment were only entitled to equitable forms of relief outlined in 42 U.S.C. Section 2000e-5(g). While equitable remedies are still available, victims now have the additional right to seek legal remedies under section 1981a.[105]

Compensatory damages, now part of Title VII's remedial scheme, include monetary compensation to the victim for such things as future pecuniary losses, emotional pain, suffering, inconvenience, mental anguish, loss of enjoyment of life, and other non-pecuniary losses caused by the harassing conduct.[106] A plaintiff may not, however, recover for the same injury under section 1981a(b) as compensatory relief, and again under section 2000e-5(g).[107] For example, a plaintiff entitled to back pay as compensatory damages and equitable relief may not receive a duplicative award. Section 1981a(a) does not specify, however, whether complaining parties are entitled to non-duplicative remedies outlined in both sections.[108]

Recently enacted section 1981a also permits a plaintiff to seek punitive damages against a defendant who acted with "malice" or "reckless indifference" when breaching the victim's federally protected right to be free from workplace harassment. By allowing recovery of such damages designed to punish and deter, rather than compensate, Congress has finally acknowledged the seriousness and prevalence of sexual harassment.

Section 1981a, however, imposes limits to the new legal remedies available to plaintiffs in a hostile environment suit. The amount of compensatory and punitive damages recoverable depends upon the number of employees a defendant employs in "each of 20 or more calendar weeks in the current or preceding calendar year."[110] Compensatory and punitive damages added together for each plaintiff cannot exceed $50,000 for a defendant with more than 14 and less than 101 employees during this period, $100,000 for a defendant with more than 100 and less than 201 employees, $200,000 for a defendant with more than 200 and less than 501 employees, and $300,000 for a defendant with more than 500 employees.[111]

Prior to November of 1991, plaintiffs bringing hostile environment sexual harassment claims under Title VII were only allowed equitable relief.[112] Reinstatement, injunctions, and equitable monetary damages such as back and front pay, nominal damages, and attorney fees and costs were the only remedies available. While compensatory and/or punitive damages may provide more adequate relief, such equitable remedies are still likely to be employed by courts when formulating remedial plans.

A plaintiff who wins her hostile environment claim is presumptively entitled to back pay if she has unlawfully been discharged, demoted, or denied promotion. Back pay is not limited to salary, but includes the value of such things as bonuses, sick leave, vacation, and other benefits. In order to collect, however, the plaintiff bears the initial burden of proving that her economic loss was a direct result of the discriminatory harassment. Economic loss claimed by the plaintiff cannot be speculative in nature, but must be compensation she would have received in the ordinary course of her employment were it not for the harasser's illegal conduct.[113] The court in *Huddleston v. Roger Dean Chevrolet, Inc.*,[114] for example, held that evidence of lost commissions was too vague to entitle the plaintiff to economic relief.

Once the plaintiff presents evidence of non-speculative lost income, the burden shifts to the employer. The employer may try to rebut the plaintiff's claim that the economic loss actually resulted from discrimination, prove its speculative nature, or question the amount. Unless the employer can prove one of these factors by a preponderance of the evidence, however, the employer will be liable for the loss.[115] If successful, a plaintiff will recover the difference between her actual earnings during the period of harassment and what she would have earned absent the defendant's unlawful conduct.[116] Where actual loss is not proven or not provable, a court may award nominal damages as a surrogate for back pay.[117]

Plaintiffs who were actually or constructively discharged, but do not seek reinstatement due to an irreparable atmosphere at work, may seek an award of front pay.[118] The burden on the plaintiff seeking front pay is similar to the burden described above; however, in seeking front pay the plaintiff may also need to show that reinstatement is not a plausible alternative. For example, in *Gross v. Exxon Office Systems Co.,*[119] the court awarded a victim of sexual harassment $12,523 in front pay under Title VII only after finding that reinstatement was impracticable because of the hostility existing between the parties. The award in *Gross* represented four months of pay, after which it was determined that the plaintiff would be able to earn as much or more as she did working for the defendant.[120]

Because compensatory and punitive damages have only recently become available to victims, the most commonly awarded remedy for hostile environment sexual harassment under Title VII has been reinstatement accompanied by an injunction to prevent continued harassment. When a plaintiff has been actually or constructively discharged as a result of sexual harassment she is entitled to reinstatement to the position she would have occupied were it not for the unlawful behavior. Reinstatement includes retroactive seniority rights as well as other fringe benefits that would have accrued.

Since reinstatement is only a viable remedy if the environment is harassment-free, courts often issue injunctions against defendants to cease and desist harassment. Injunctions can also ensure that harassment does not resume. Such relief may include an order for the employer to adopt a meaningful policy against sexual harassment as well as an effective complaint procedure.

Finally, section 2000e-5(k) enables courts to award reasonable attorney fees to prevailing parties. This provision, along with the legislature's decision to allow limited recovery of compensatory and punitive damages in sexual harassment cases, provides necessary impetus for the enforcement of Title VII.

Unfortunately, before the 1991 amendment, most victims of

workplace harassment tried to ignore, endure, or escape their harassers, instead of taking them to court. Even today, many victims continue to employ these techniques, after weighing the monetary and emotional costs of litigation, as well as the likelihood that they may face discrimination at the hands of the legal system. The trouble with these alternative responses is that ignoring and enduring may cost victims their autonomy, self-esteem, psychological well-being, and eventually their jobs. Considering the competition women face in the labor market and the prevalence of harassment in all sectors, escape is also not an easy feat.

K. DISCOVERY AND EVIDENCE

Several evidentiary issues of crucial importance to plaintiffs in a hostile environment case have yet to be resolved by the courts. Only on the issue of the admissibility of plaintiffs' sexually provocative speech and dress is there word from the Supreme Court. According to the court in *Meritor,* the plaintiff's sexually provocative speech or dress is "obviously" relevant in determining whether she found her supervisor's sexual advances unwelcome.[121] "While the District Court must carefully weigh the applicable considerations in deciding whether to admit evidence of this kind," the Supreme court held, "there is no per se rule against its admissibility."[122]

The Supreme Court has not made any such statements about the admissibility of plaintiffs' sexual history in sexual harassment cases. Lower courts, however, have held that information about a plaintiff's sexual history and off-work conduct is not discoverable. The court in *Priest v. Rotary,*[123] for instance, held that evidence of an individual's prior acts is not admissible to prove that she engaged in similar conduct on a particular occasion.[124] To get around this holding the defendant in *Priest* argued that he was seeking the names of each person the plaintiff had sexual relations with in the last ten years to demonstrate that the plaintiff was fired not for refusing her supervisor's sexual come-ons, but for flirting with the customers. According to the defendant, this evidence would show that she had a habit of living with men to derive economic benefits from them. The court characterized this argument as "a thinly disguised attempt to seek character evidence" and upheld the district court's decision to grant plaintiff's protective order.[125]

The court in *Priest* perceptively points out that courts should learn from their experience in rape trials that sexual harassment plaintiffs require protection from intimidation and discouragement if their statutory claim is to have any real meaning. According to the court:

> [E]mployees whose intimate lives are unjustifiably and offensively intruded upon in the workplace might face the "Catch-22" of invoking their statutory remedy only at the risk of enduring further intrusions into irrelevant details of their personal lives. . . . By carefully examining our experience with rape prosecutions, however, the courts and bar can avoid repeating in this new field of civil sexual harassment suits the same mistakes that are now being corrected in the rape context.[126]

The Catch-22 the court speaks of, unfortunately, is difficult to avoid where stereotypes and old-fashioned notions of female sexuality cloud the assessment of relevance and undue prejudice.

There is a long history in this country of ignoring or downplaying injuries experienced by a woman on the notion that "she asked for it." The double standard that makes it okay for men to boast of their sexual exploits and brands women as "sluts" or "whores" for their sexual experiences must carefully be brought to light when arguing relevance and prejudice issues in regard to evidence about dress, fantasy, or prior sexual history in a hostile environment case. While the addition of section 412[127] to the Federal Rules of Evidence may indicate a growing understanding of gender bias in evidentiary determinations, such guidance applies only to rape cases and has not been extended to sexual harassment cases, despite the similar circumstances.

In sexual harassment cases, as in rape cases, the alleged conduct is often witnessed only by the parties themselves and credibility is the deciding factor. Since appellate courts view the trial courts' determination of credibility issues with deference, the admissibility of corroborating evidence is especially important to plaintiffs bringing a hostile environment claim. Not all courts agree, however, that testimony from other employees who have been harassed by the same individual is admissible to corroborate a plaintiff's claim. According to the Fifth Circuit in *Jones v. Flagship Int'l,*[128] incidents of sexual harassment reported by other female employees "though relevant in a class action suit, does not bear on Jones' individual claim of sexual harassment in the absence of evidence that such incidents affected Jones' psychological well-being." Several other courts, however, have admitted testimony of other women victimized by the same harasser.[129]

In *Robinson*, for example, the court explains that the testimony other female co-workers is relevant to rebut the assertion that the conduct of which Robinson complained was isolated or rare. In addition, Robinson's perception of her work environment as hostile may have been influenced by the treatment that other similarly situated co-workers were experiencing. Finally, the court recognized that instances of sexual harassment of other women is relevant to the issue of employer liability since it makes the proposition that the employer knew or should have known of the hostile environment more likely.[130]

L. RELATED CLAIMS

Although this guide focuses on the hostile environment claim under federal statutory law, there are other claims that may be brought by women who are victims of sexual harassment at work. Disillusioned by the inadequate damages provided by Title VII to victims of sexual harassment prior to November 1991, many states have adopted their own fair employment laws which allow for compensatory and punitive damage awards. In addition, there are related state and federal employment discrimination, criminal, and common law claims that hostile environment plaintiffs can bring against their harassers and/or employers.

Claims that plaintiffs should consider include: quid pro quo sexual harassment, racial harassment, sex discrimination, constructive discharge, retaliatory discharge, wrongful termination in violation of public policy, negligent hiring or supervision, negligent misrepresentation, breach of covenant of good faith and fair dealing, breach of contract, intentional or negligent interference with contractual relationship, intentional or negligent infliction of emotional distress, defamation, fraud, false imprisonment, assault, battery, and rape.

NOTES

1. Safran, *What Men Do to Women on the Job: A Shocking Look at Sexual Harassment*, REDBOOK 149, 217-223 (November 1976).

2. *Sexual Harassment in the Federal Government: Hearings Before the House Committee on Post Office and Civil Service*, 96th Cong., 1st Sess. 1(1979).

3. Corne v. Bausch & Lomb, 390 F. Supp. 161 (D. Ariz. 1975), *vacated* and *remanded*, apparently on issue of referral to state agency, 562 F.2d 55 (9th Cir. 1977). According to Catharine MacKinnon, Barnes v. Train, 13 FEP Cases 123 (D.D.C. 1974) was the first sexual harassment case decided, but was reported after Corne. C. MACKINNON, SEXUAL HARASSMENT OF WORKING WOMEN 60 (1979).

4. Corne, 390 F. Supp. at 163.

5. 413 F. Supp. 654 (D.D.C. 1976); *remanded*, for trial de novo because lower court's review of administrative record was not sufficient to sustain the judgment, 587 F.2d 1240, 1241-42 (D.C. Cir. 1978).

6. *Id.* at 657-58.

7. 561 F.2d 983 (D.C. Cir. 1977).

8. *Id.* at 994-95.

9. *E.g.*, Rogers v. EEOC, 454 F.2d 234 (5th Cir. 1971), *cert. denied*, 406 U.S. 957 (1972).

10. *Id.* at 238.

11. *E.g..,* Compston v. Borden, Inc. 424 F. Supp 157 (S.D. Ohio 1976) (religion); Cariddi v. Kansas City Chiefs' Football Club, 568 F.2d 87 (8th Cir. 1977)(national origin).

12. Bundy v. Jackson, 641 F.2d 934 (D.C. Cir. 1981).

13. 682 F.2d 897, 902 (11th Cir. 1982).

14. Meritor, 477 U.S. at 67.

15. 42 U.S.C. §2000e-2(a)(1).

16. 477 U.S. at 62. Although the court distinguishes between quid pro quo and hostile environment, the claims may overlap. For instance, if an employee's environment was so hostile that she was constructively discharged, she can argue that compliance with unwelcome sexual behavior that created the hostile environment was a quid pro quo of her continued employment. Since employer liability is analyzed according to different standards in quid pro quo and hostile environment cases, this overlap is important to keep in mind. *EEOC: Policy Guidance on Sexual Harassment*, [Fair Empl. Prac. Manual] Lab. Rel. Rep (BNA) 405:6681, 6682 [hereinafter *Policy Guidance Memorandum*], (the *Policy Guidance Memorandum* is a procedural handbook that was issued by the Commission to its field office personnel in 1990).

17. According to the Equal Employment Opportunity Commission, the central inquiry is whether the conduct unreasonably interferes with an individual's work performance *or* creates an intimidating, hostile, or offensive working environment. 29 C.F.R. §1604.11(a)(3)(1992). The EEOC states that despite federal court findings that require a showing of psychological injury, "it is the Commission's position that it is sufficient for the charging party to show that the harassment was unwelcome and that it would have substantially affected the work environment of a reasonable person." *Policy Guidance Memorandum, supra,* note 16 at 405:6690, n.20.

The Sixth Circuit has twice indicated, however, that a plaintiff may not prevail on a hostile environment claim without proving that the conduct complained of affected the individual's work performance *and* her psychological well-being. Rabidue v. Osceola Refining Co., 805 F.2d 611, 620 (6th Cir. 1986 *cert. denied,* 481 U.S. 1041 (1987), Highlander v. K.F.C. Nat'l Management Co., 805 F.2d 644, 650 (6th Cir. 1986). At present the Sixth Circuit is the only one that has adopted this dual requirement.

18. 42 U.S.C. §2000e-5.

19. 29 C.F.R. §1604.11(a)(1992).

20. 477 U.S. at 65.

21. 42 U.S.C. §2000e-2(a)(1).

22. Meritor, 477 U.S. at 68.

23. *Id.*

24. 682 F.2d at 903.

25. *Policy Guidance Memorandum, supra,* note 16, at 405:6685.

26. *Id.*

27. *Id.*

28. *Id.*

29. *Id.* at 405:6686.

30. *Id.*

31. Henson, 682 F.2d at 904.

32. 760 F. Supp. 1486, (M.D. Fla. 1991). At the time the final manuscript for this book was due, this case had been appealed, but no decision had yet been handed down.

33. *Id.* at 1522. *See also,* Andrews v. City of Philadelphia, 895 F.2d 1469, 1485 (3rd. Cir. 1990) ("The offensive conduct is not necessarily required to include sexual overtones in every instance.") Hall v. Gus Construction Co., 842 F.2d 1010, 1014 (8th Cir. 1988) ("Intimidation and hostility toward women because they are women can obviously result from conduct other than sexual advances.")

34. 760 F. Supp at 1523.

35. *Id.* at 1522. *E.g.,* Huddleston v. Roger Dean Chevrolet, Inc., 845 F.2d 900, 904-05 (11th Cir. 1988); Sparks v. Pilot Freight Carriers, *Inc.,* 830 F.2d 1554, 1561 (11th Cir. 1987).

36. Robinson, 760 F. Supp. at 1522-23. *See* Henson, 682 F.2d at 904; *see also* Andrews, 895 F.2d at 1485-86 and Lipsett v. Univ. of Puerto Rico, 864 F.2d 881, 905 (1st Cir. 1988).

37. Robinson, 760 F. Supp. at 1523.

38. *See, e.g.,* Rabidue, 805 F.2d at 620.

39. Ellison v. Brady, 924 F.2d 872, 878 (9th Cir. 1991); Andrews, 895 F.2d at 1482; Yates v. Avco, Corp., 819 F.2d 630, 637 (6th Cir. 1987); Rabidue, 805 F.2d at 626 (Keith, J., *dissenting*).

40. Rabidue, 805 F.2d at 626.

41. Ellison, 924 F.2d at 879.

42. *Id.* at 880.

43. *Id.* at 879.

44. Rabidue, 805 F.2d at 620.

45. *Id.* at 620; *See also*, Robinson, 760 F. Supp at 1524 ("The objective evaluation must account for the salient conditions of the work environment, such as the rarity of women in the relevant work areas.").

46. This hypothetical was posed to me by Barbara Bryant who instructed a sexual harassment course at Boalt Hall School of Law, University of California, Berkeley, in the Fall of 1991.

47. *See, e.g.,* Henson, 682 F.2d at 904.

48. Ross v. Double Diamond, Inc., 672 F. Supp. 261, 270-71 (N.D. Tex. 1987).

49. *See, e.g, Id.* at 270.

50. Robin Lakoff, author of *Language and Woman's Place* (Octagon Books, 1976, and *Talking Power: The Politics of Language in Our Lives* (Basic Books, 1990), introduced me to this idea of the multiple meanings of language during a lecture she gave for a seminar on sexual harassment I was enrolled in at Boalt Hall School of Law in the Fall of 1991. She used this example of pornography as an illustration.

51. Rabidue, 805 F.2d at 620-21.

52. *See e.g.,* Priest v. Rotary 634 F. Supp. 571 (N.D. Cal. 1986) (When plaintiff's supervisor put his arms around her, put his hands on her breasts, kissed her neck, trapped her between himself and another male employee, exposed his genitals to her, and fondled other female employees in her presence, conduct cannot be considered isolated or trivial, but is part of an ongoing pattern of harassing behavior); Ambrose v. U.S. Steel Corp., 39 FEP 30 (N.D. Cal. 1985) (Supervisor's flirtatious overtures, attempts to kiss her, and inquiry into her past experiences with oral sex were enough to demonstrate ongoing pattern of harassment).

53. *Policy Guidance Memorandum, supra,* note 16 at 405:6690.

54. *See, e.g.,* Rabidue, 805 F.2d at 622 (Plaintiff's well-being not seriously affected by posters of nude women displayed in her work environment and obscene and sexist comments consistently made to her by her male supervisor); Henson, 682 F.2d at 905 (Plaintiff subjected to harassment sufficiently severe to state a claim when chief of her police department makes repeated requests for sex over two-year period); Ellison, 924 F.2d at 880 (After continually asking plaintiff out despite her refusals, writing her a note expressing his attraction to her which was followed by a three-page letter, the mere presence of the harasser was sufficiently severe and pervasive to create an abusive working environment).

55. The *National Law Journal* in conjunction with West Publishing Co. con-

ducted a survey of 900 female attorneys at 56 large law firms. The results indicated that 60% were subjected to unwanted sexual attention. Thirteen women reported that they were victims of actual or attempted rape and assaults by their superiors. The survey also indicates that women rarely reported incidents of unwelcome behavior and of those who did, 56% said that the firm did nothing., Couric, *Women in the Law Firms: A High Price of Admission? Nat.L.J.,* December 11, 1989, at S2.

56. Vinson v. Taylor, 753 F.2d 141, 146 (D.C. Cir. 1985) *aff'd,* 477 U.S. 57.

57. 42 U.S.C. §2000e (b). Plaintiffs will also be able to hold their harassers personally liable under Title VII if they are considered agents of the employer. *E.g.,* Robinson, 760 F. Supp at 151.

58. *Policy Guidance Memorandum, supra* note 16 at 405:6682, 405:6694.

59. *Id.,* at 405:6682.

60. *Id.,* at 405:6695-99.

61. 477 U.S. at 72.

62. *Id.*

63. *Id.*

64. *Id.* at 73.

65. *Id.*

66. *Policy Guidance Memorandum, supra,* note 16 at 405:6695; EEOC v. Hacienda Hotel, 881 F.2d 1504, 1515-16 (9th Cir. 1989).

67. *Policy Guidance Memorandum, supra,* note 16 at 405:6695.

68. Henson, 682 F.2d at 905.

69. *Policy Guidance Memorandum, supra,* note 16 at 405:6700.

70. *Id.,* Ellison, 924 F.2d at 881-82.

71. *Policy Guidance Memorandum, supra,* note 16 at 405:6700.

72. *Id.*

73. *Id.,* Ellison, 924 F.2d at 882.

74. *Policy Guidance Memorandum, supra,* note 16 at 405:6700.

75. Barrett v. Omaha Nat'l Bank, 726 F.2d 424, 427 (8th Cir. 1984) (Court finds that employer's response to victim's complaint is prompt and appropriate where, within four days after complaint, employer investigated charges, placed guilty employee on probation and warned him that future misconduct would result in discharge).

76. Brooms v. Regal Tube Co., 881 F.2d 412, 421 (7th Cir. 1989).

77. *Policy Guidance Memorandum, supra,* note 16 at 405:6696-97.

78. RESTATEMENT (SECOND) OF AGENCY §219(1) (Am. Law. Inst. Pub., 1958).

79. *EEOC Policy Guidance Memorandum, supra,* note 16 at 405:6696-97.

80. *Id.* at 405:6697.

81. *Id.;* RESTATEMENT (SECOND) OF AGENCY, *supra,* note 78 §§7,8,219(2)(d).

82. *Policy Guidance Memorandum, supra* note 16 at 405:6697.

83. *Id.*

84. *Id.* at 405:6698; Hicks v. Gates Rubber Co., 833 F.2d 1406, 1418 (10th Cir. 1987) Court remands case and lower court's decision in favor of employer is affirmed in 928 F.2d 966 (10th Cir. 1991).

85. 477 U.S. at 65.

86. *Policy Guidance Memorandum, supra,* note 16 at 405:6699; RESTATEMENT (SECOND) OF AGENCY, *supra,* note 78 §219(2)(c).

87. 44 FEP Cases 1119, 1124 (N.D. Ill. 1987), *aff'd on other ground,* 881 F.2d 412 (7th Cir. 1989).

88. RESTATEMENT (SECOND) OF AGENCY, *supra,* note 78, §219(2)(d).

89. 830 F.2d at 1554, 1560.

90. 477 U.S. at 76. (J. Marshall *concurring,* joined by J J. Brennan, Blackmun, and Stevens).

91. *Id.* at 76-77. *See also,* Rabidue, 805 F.2d at 625 (J. Keith, *dissenting*).

92. DFEH v. Del Mar Avionics and Coy Wall, FEHC No. 85-19 at 25 (1985).

93. 29 C.F.R. §1604.11(d) (1992). Note that this standard applies to co-workers as well as non-employees such as customers, vendors, and independent contractors. 29 C.F.R. §1604.11(e).

94. Look for upcoming decisions to address the issue of the First Amendment as a defense to sexual harassment claims.

95. 42 U.S.C. §2000e-5(e).

96. 42 U.S.C. §2000e-5(c). For list of states that have either state or local agencies which the EEOC defers to, see 21 Fed. Proc. JOB DISCRIMINATION §50:6 [1984].

97. 42 U.S.C. §2000e-5(c).

98. *Id.*

99. *Id.*

100. 29 C.F.R. §1601.13(a)(4)(i)(1992); Love v. Pullman Co., 404 U.S. 522 (1972).

101. 29 C.F.R. §1601.13(a)(1)(1992), 29 C.F.R. §1601.13(a)(2), *See, generally, Sufficiency of state remedy under 42 USCS §2000e-5(c) to require 60-day deferral by Equal Employment Opportunity Commission to allow state time to act,* 45 A.L.R. Fed. 347 [1979].

102. 42 U.S.C. 2000e-5(e).

103. 667 F.2d 788, 790 (9th Cir. 1982).

104. 42 U.S.C. 1981a.

105. Note that whenever a plaintiff seeks compensatory or punitive damages in a hostile environment suit, either party may demand a trial by jury. 42 U.S.C. 1981a(c).

106. 42 U.S.C. 1981a(b)(3).

107. 42 U.S.C. 1981a(b)(2).

108. 42 U.S.C. 1981a(a).

109. 42 U.S.C. 1981a(b)(1).

110. 42 U.S.C. 1981a(3)(A)-(D).

111. *Id.*

112. 42 U.S.C. 2000e-5(g).

113. *See, e.g.,* Jinks v. Mays, 464 F.2d 1223, 1226 (5th Cir. 1972) (Proving wages are properly owed "requires positive proof that plaintiff was ordinarily entitled to the wages in question and, being without fault, would have received them

in the ordinary course of things but for the inequitable conduct of the party from whom the wages are claimed.").

114. 845 F.2d 900, 905 (11th Cir. 1988).

115. Robinson, 760 F. Supp. at 1533.

116. Horn v. Duke Homes, 755 F.2d 599, 606 (7th Cir. 1985).

117. Huddleston, 845 F.2d at 905; Henson, 682 F.2d at 905; Robinson, 760 F. Supp. at 1533.

118. Nord v. United Steel Corp., 758 F.2d 1462, 1473 (11th Cir. 1985)

119. 747 F.2d 885, 889-90 (3rd Cir. 1984).

120. *Id.*

121. 477 U.S. at 69.

122. *Id.*

123. 98 F.R.D. 755, 758 (N.D. Calif. 1983).

124. Fed. Rules of Evid., 28 U.S.C. §404(a).

125. Priest, 98 F.R.D. at 759.

126. *Id.* at 761-762.

127. Fed. R. Evid. §412 limits the use of evidence of the victim's past sexual behavior in criminal rape trials.

128. 793 F.2d 714, 721 n.7 (5th Cir. 1986).

129. Yates, 819 F.2d at 635-36.

130. Robinson, 760 F. Supp. at 1499.

III. Research Tools

Legal research is largely a matter of sex, drugs, and rock 'n' roll. Well, not really, but at least we have caught your attention.

JOHNSON, BERRING, AND WOXLAND, WINNING RESEARCH SKILLS, 1 (1991)

The purpose of this book is to make sexual harassment law accessible to anyone interested: lawyers, scholars, victims, and employers alike. Toward this end, this chapter takes into account the interests of those who have never had the pleasure of doing legal research.[1] The following suggestions for research tools, indexing terms, and short cuts, however, will save even experienced legal researchers time (i.e., money) and frustration. Databases and looseleaf services are the most efficient tools for doing legal research on the hostile environment claim. Special libraries are the best for finding books, articles, and other popular treatments of the subject.

A. WHERE TO BEGIN

The best place to begin your research depends, of course, on what you are looking for. Someone unfamiliar with hostile environment sexual harassment might start by reading Part II of this guide. Also good for an overview of the hostile environment claim is *When is work environment intimidating, hostile, or offensive, so as to constitute sexual harassment in violation of Title VII of Civil Rights Act of 1964, as amended (42 U.S.C.S.§§2000e et seq.)*, 78 A.L.R. Fed. 252. For an even briefer description, see *Job Discrimination* 45A Am. Jur. 2nd §781.

On the other hand, someone who has a basic understanding of the claim, but is looking for something in particular (a brief, case, or law review article on a certain issue, for example), will find that the table of contents to this book is a good place to start. If the information is not contained in the book itself, the guidelines below will help you in your search.

B. DATABASE SERVICES

The databases are outstanding research tools because they enable researchers to find statutes, regulations, cases, briefs, articles, annotations, and more all in one place. When information is especially difficult to find through a bound index (e.g., the text of a congressional floor debate), the ability to conduct a full-text database search is especially valuable. It is also better to update information on-line since the services are kept more current than paper services. Although reading through cases or law review articles on-line can be time-consuming and expensive, the databases make it possible to print citation lists of sources on point. Such lists make it easy for researchers to locate the information on paper. Those who have access to the major database services should consider the suggestions that follow.

1. LEXIS[2]

LEXIS is a convenient tool for researching the hostile environment claim. LEXIS is especially time-saving since many of the bound indexes, such as West's *Federal Digest, 4th* and the periodical indexes, do not use "Hostile Environment" as a subheading under "Sexual Harassment." For a narrow search on the hostile environment claim use "hostile w/5 environment w/50 woman." For a broader search use "sex! w/10 harass! w/50 woman." Good files to search include the following:

a. ALR. ANNO. For annotations from *A.L.R. (2nd, 3rd, 4th & Fed.) and Lawyers Ed. 2nd.*

b. BNA. DLABRT. For *Daily Labor Report* starting January, 1982.

BNA. FEPOUT. For BNA's *Labor Relations Reporter Fair Employment Practice Cases Outline of Classifications.*

BNA. IERNEW. For BNA's *Labor Relations Reporter Individual Employment Rights Newsletter* starting September, 1986

BNA. LRRFEP. For BNA's *Labor Relations Reporter Fair Employment Practice Cases* starting with volume 1, 1969.

BNA. USLW. For *United States Law Week* starting July, 1982.

c. EMPLOY. ADMIN. For employment-related decisions including those from the EEOC and NLRB beginning January, 1970.

EMPLOY. COURTS. For employment-related case law from federal courts.

EMPLOY. EEOMAN. For the *EEOC Compliance Manual,* volumes I and II.

EMPLOY. (Supply two-letter state code). For employment decisions in a particular state.

d. GENFED. BRIEFS. For briefs filed in United States Supreme Court cases beginning October, 1979.

e. LABOR. COURTS. For all federal court decisions involving labor issues.

LABOR. EEOC. For the text of EEOC decisions since January of 1970.

f. LAWREV. ALLREV. For law review articles.

g. LEXREF. ILP. For H. W. Wilson's *Index to Legal Periodicals.*

LEXREF. LEGLIND. For Information Access Company's *Legal Resource Index.*

2. WESTLAW[3]

Like LEXIS, WESTLAW also allows you to do an on-line full-text search to find just hostile environment cases, rather than sexual harassment cases in general. The most important thing to remember about WESTLAW and LEXIS is that they have different information on-line. Using either database can create the illusion that you are accessing all relevant sources, but this is not the case. For example, WESTLAW and LEXIS do not have all over the same law reviews and journals on-line.[4]

The best narrow search on WESTLAW is "hostile /s environment /p woman." The best broad search is "sex! /s harass! /p woman." Good databases to search include:

a. BNA-DLR. For BNA's *Daily Labor Report* starting in 1986.

b. FLB-ALL. For all federal labor materials including court decisions, codes, and regulations.

   FLB-CS. For all federal labor-related decisions.

   FLB-EEOC. For EEOC decisions since 1969.

c. ILP. For H. W. Wilson's *Index to Legal Periodicals.*

d. JLR. For all journal and law review articles.

e. LB-TP. For labor texts and periodicals.

f. LRI. For Information Access Company's *Legal Resource Index*, 1980.

g. (Supply two-letter state code). LB-CS. For labor case law from a particular state.

h. NEWSEARCH. For index of news stories, informational articles, and book reviews.

i. NLJ. For the *National Law Journal* beginning October, 1989.

j. WTH-LB. For WESTLAW topical highlights on employment law.

3. NEXIS[5]

NEXIS is an on-line service that includes secondary sources of information such as newspapers, popular magazines, and professional journals. NEXIS allows researchers to do a full-text search of sources like *Los Angeles Times, New York Times, Chicago Tribune, Sacramento Bee, U.S. News and World Report, Working Woman, Legal Times, American Lawyer,* and *National Law Journal.*

A good file to search is NEXIS. CURRNT, which includes stories from all full-text files in the NEXIS library published after 1989. Another good file to search is NEXIS. LGLNEW, which includes the legal news publications mentioned above. The search "woman w/50 harass! and sex!" brings up sexual harassment stories. A more limited search incorporating the terms "hostile" and "environment" might exclude relevant information.

C. DIGEST SERVICES

The best digest of federal court cases on the hostile environment claim is *West's Federal Practice Digest, 4th.* Hostile environment cases are included under the heading "Civil Rights - 167, Harassment; work environment." Because West does not give "Hostile Environment" its own keynumber, it is necessary to skim all the summaries of sexual harassment decisions to find the ones brought on a hostile environment claim. This is especially frustrating because of the sheer amount of cases categorized under the general heading. A good way to find recent cases, however, is to check the paper supplement to this digest.

Database and looseleaf services are better tools to use to find cases on the hostile environment claim. Citations in law review and journal articles are another quick way to find cites to cases on point. For citations to recent cases, also check the pocket part supplements in *Sex Discrimination: Sexual Harassment, Creating a Hostile Work Environment,* 50 Am Jur POF 2nd 127, and *When is work environment intimidating, hostile, or offensive, so as to constitute sexual harassment in violation of Title VII of Civil Rights Act of 1964, as amended (42 U.S.C.S. §§2000 et seq.),* 78 A.L.R Fed. 252.

D. LOOSELEAF SERVICES

Like databases, looseleaf services are especially useful when researching the hostile environment claim because they bring statutes, regulations, cases, digest materials, policy statements, and other background information together in one place. Since the biggest services are available at most public law libraries, the price of using a looseleaf service is also right. Listed below are the best and most readily available services helpful in researching the hostile environment claim. The sheer amount of information included in some of the bigger looseleafs makes the indexing complex and somewhat difficult to decipher, so it is best to pick one service and stick to it. There is no need to waste time familiarizing yourself with the workings of each service.

Arlene L. Eis's *Legal Looseleafs in Print* (Infosources Publishing, 1992) lists looseleaf services according to subject. Although law libraries cannot afford to subscribe to all of these services, you should be able to find one from *Legal Looseleafs in Print* that is available at a local library. *Legal Looseleafs in Print* lists services that are relevant to the hostile environment claim under the topics "Discrimination," "Civil Rights," "Women's Rights," and "Labor and Labor Relations." "Sexual Harassment" is a good term to use when looking up information in the services themselves. Look for "Hostile Environment" to be listed as a subtopic.

1. Personal Favorites

a. *Employment Coordinator* (Research Institute of America).

This service has especially good indexing. Since RIA is more selective in what it publishes, it is easy to find information on point in *Employment Coordinator*. Volume eight of the 15-volume *Employment Practices* set includes information on the hostile environment claim. Especially useful in this service is a summarization of state laws prohibiting sexual harassment. Information on sexual harassment in employment is indexed under EP-22,201.

b. *Labor Relations Reporter* (BNA).

This service is broken down into many parts, including *Analysis News and Background Information, State Laws, Fair Employment Practices Manual, Fair Employment Practice Cases, Individual Employment Rights Manual, Individual*

Rights Cases, Labor Arbitration, and *Labor Relations Expediter.*

Fair Empl. Prac. Manual, for example, contains policy statements on the hostile environment claim. *Fair Empl. Prac. Cases* contains the full text of hostile environment decisions. BNA's *Fair Empl. Prac. Index* is therefore the best way to access relevant information in this service. Although this service is comparable to CCH's *Labor Law Reporter,* it is somewhat easier to find information on the hostile environment claim in BNA's service. Both the BNA and CCH looseleafs provide broad coverage of the subject.

2. Also Good

a. *Daily Labor Report* (BNA).

This service does not include the full text of statutes and cases, but does include, among other things, information on labor issues put out by administrative agencies. *Daily Labor Report* is updated daily and is also available on-line.

b. *EEOC Compliance Manual* (CCH).

This manual is a practical guide for employers to facilitate compliance with EEOC regulations. The manual does not include anything on the hostile environment claim which cannot be found in the more comprehensive services listed above. Nevertheless, *EEOC Compliance Manual* is listed here because it provides more information pertinent to the claim than comparable manuals offered by other publishers. For information on the EEOC's sexual harassment regulations see ¶3100-3105.

c. *Labor Law Reporter* (CCH).

Like BNA's *Labor Relations Reporter,* CCH's *Labor Law Reporter* assembles the text of statues, regulations, decisions, and policy statements in one service. *Labor Law Reporter* is a valuable tool for hostile environment research, but somewhat more difficult to use than BNA's service.

E. LEGAL PERIODICAL INDEXES

Legal periodicals are perhaps the best source of information on the hostile environment claim. Unfortunately, locating periodical literature on point is time-consuming due to the bulk of data contained in the indexes. Looking for the most current articles requires the use of a supplement or two. Looking for articles published over a longer period of time, however, requires looking up your search term in many volumes. Slowing the process even more is the fact that articles on the hostile environment claim are listed under the index heading "Sexual Harassment." It is often impossible to tell from the title of the article whether or not its contents address the hostile environment claim. This may make it necessary to locate and skim numerous articles in order to find what you are looking for.

Many libraries have computerized indexing services. These services allow you to find every article categorized under your term at once, avoiding a year-by-year search. Unfortunately, such systems do not overcome the fact that articles on the hostile environment claim will be grouped together with articles on sexual harassment in general. Only databases like LEXIS and WESTLAW, which store the text of many periodicals on-line, circumvent this problem by allowing you to conduct full-text searches for particular terms. Databases are therefore the quickest, though definitely not the cheapest, way to go. In addition, neither LEXIS or WESTLAW includes the text of all legal periodicals on-line.

For these reasons, there is no best way to find legal periodicals on the hostile environment claim. Some of the better tools to try are listed below.

1. LEXIS

To do a full-text search of legal articles in periodical publications use LAWREV. ALLREV. The best narrow search for materials on the hostile environment claim is "hostile w/5 environment w/50 woman." The best broad search is "sex! w/10 harass! w/50 woman."

2. NEXIS

Using NEXIS. LGLNEW it is possible to do a full-text search of legal newspapers including *National Law Journal, Legal Times*, and *American Lawyer.* Since newspaper articles tend to be more general, the search "sex w/10 harass! w/50 woman" is a good one to try.

3. WESTLAW

A full-text search in LB-TP will locate all labor-related articles in legal periodicals containing your search terms. To search for legal news articles from *National Law Journal* use the NLJ file. The best narrow search to run on WESTLAW is "hostile /s environment /p woman." The best broad search is "sex! /s harass! /p woman." Remember that the periodicals contained on WESTLAW are different than on LEXIS, and neither includes the entire field of legal periodical literature.

4. *Current Law Index*

Current Law Index is available in bound volumes and on-line. On LEXIS and WESTLAW, this Information Access Corporation service is called *Legal Resource Index.* Articles on the hostile environment claim are indexed under "Sexual Harassment of Women."

5. *Index to Legal Periodicals*

This H. W. Wilson publication is available in bound volumes and on LEXIS and WESTLAW. Look for hostile environment articles under the index term "Sexual Harassment."

6. *Legal Newsletters in Print*, Arlene L. Eis, Ed.

Legal Newsletters in Print, published by Infosources Publishing, lists newsletters in print and tells you how to subscribe. Small and large newsletters from across the nation, some on very specific topics, are included. While there is no sexual harassment newsletter to date, *Legal Newsletters in Print* does include many newsletters addressed to working women. Note, however, that this publication is not an index of articles in newsletters, but only a list of newsletter titles. The best search terms to use in the subject index are "Discrimination" and "Women's Rights."

F. POPULAR PERIODICAL INDEXES

Articles in popular periodicals are more likely to deal in general with sexual harassment at work, rather than with the hostile environment claim in particular. Nevertheless, such articles may include useful statistics on sexual harassment and cover court cases as well as newly proposed laws. Unfortunately, the same problems with locating relevant articles in legal periodicals, discussed above, are accentuated by the sheer bulk of information contained in the popular indexes. Look for libraries that have computerized periodical indexes to speed your search. The tools to use for locating popular periodical literature on sexual harassment include the following:

1. NEXIS

NEXIS allows researchers to do full-text searches in many, but not all, popular periodicals. It is an expensive service and is not available to many researchers. Those who have the luxury of using NEXIS, however, can search all the major newspapers and many popular magazines for sexual harassment stories in NEXIS. CURRNT. The best search to conduct is "woman w/50 harass! and sex!"

2. WESTLAW

NEWSEARCH is a database index of news stories, informational articles, and book reviews which is worth searching for popular treatment of the subject if you have access to WEST-LAW.

3. *Reader's Guide to Periodical Literature*

This H. W. Wilson publication is available at any public library and usually available in a computerized version.

4. Newspaper Indexes

The New York Times Company publishes a bound index of all *New York Times* articles entitled *New York Times Index*. Other major papers publish similar indexes. For accumulated listings of articles in many major papers use Information Access Company's *National Newspaper Index*.

5. *Gale Directory of Publications, 119th Ed.*

Gale Research Co.'s directory includes listings of many periodicals in print. Like *Legal Newsletters in Print*, this directory lists the titles of publications, rather than articles. *Gale Directory of Publications* includes popular as well as legal periodicals.

G. SPECIAL LIBRARIES

Finding the right library is the first thing a researcher should do. A law library may be sufficient to meet your research needs. Popular treatment of the issue of sexual harassment at work, however, is often necessary to supplement legal knowledge of the claim. When this is the case, the best place to go is to a library that specializes in the topic. Women's libraries often contain the most valuable information on sexual harassment in the workplace. Many college campuses have women's resource centers which subscribe to specialized newsletters and even collect their own data kept on file. To find a specialized library near you, look up "women - employment" in the *Directory of Special Libraries and Information Centers, 16th Ed., Vol. 1* (Gale Research, Inc., 1992). Also good to check is the *American Library Directory, 45th Ed.* (R. R. Bowker's Database Publishing Group, 1992).

H. ORGANIZATIONS

Sexual harassment of women in the workplace is becoming an increasingly popular topic of interest among academics, professionals, and women's organizations. Researchers can receive precious knowledge from experts in the field who are willing to answer questions directly, provide references to current sources, and share their own findings or experiences. Below are the names, phone numbers, and addresses of organizations that employ such experts. Talking to one of them is likely to be more effective than hours of library research.

1. Government Organizations

For the names, phone numbers, and addresses of EEOC attorneys at field offices in your area, consult the *Federal Yellow Book (A Directory of The Federal Departments & Agencies), Vol. XXXII, No. 2* (Monitor Publishing Co., 1992).

EEOC
1801 L Street, N.W.
Washington, DC 20507

Public information: 202-663-4001

2. Women's Organizations

To locate legal, labor, or women's organizations in your area that may have information to share regarding sexual harassment in the workplace or the hostile environment claim, consult the *Encyclopedia of Associations, 27th Ed.* (Gale Research Inc., 1992). Below are the names of some organizations that focus on women's issues. *Encyclopedia of Associations*, however, lists many others. The organizations listed below devote resources to programs, studies, and publications aimed at solving the problem of sexual harassment of women in the workplace.

a. NOW Legal Defense and Education Fund
  99 Hudson Street
  New York, NY 10013

Phone: 212-925-6635
FAX: 212-226-1066

Contact: Alison Wetherfield, Director, Legal Program

The attorneys at NOW Legal Defense and Education Fund are working on the problem of sexual harassment in the workplace by representing victimized women and conducting extensive research on the topic. NOW publishes a legal resource kit on sexual harassment in employment, as well as *Effective Complaint and Investigation Procedures for Workplace Sexual Harassment.*

b. National Women's Law Center
   1616 P Street, N.W.
   Washington, DC 20036

   Phone: 202-328-5160
   FAX: 202-328-5137

   Contacts: Brenda Smith, Ellen Vargyas, and Marcia Greenberger, Attorneys

   Through litigation and public education, National Women's Law Center hopes to secure change for women in America. The National Women's Law Center publishes an informational article entitled *Understanding Sexual Harassment* and a legal study entitled *Title VII's Failed Promise: The Impact of the Lack of a Damages Remedy.*

c. Nine To Five, National Association of Working Women
   614 Superior Ave., N.W.
   Cleveland, OH 44113

   Phone: 216-566-9308

   Contact: Karen Nussbaum, Executive Director

   Nine To Five is an organization dedicated to gaining respect for American office workers. Part of their goal is to put a stop to the problem of sexual harassment in the workplace.

d. Wider Opportunities for Women
   1325 G Street, N.W.
   Washington, DC 20005

Phone: 202-638-3143

Contact: Cindy Marano, Executive Director

Wider Opportunities for Women is an organization designed to secure economic power for women. Their newsletter is called *Women At Work*.

e. Women Employed
    22 West Monroe, Suite 1400
    Chicago, IL 60603

Phone: 312-782-3902

Contact: Melissa Josephs, Policy Associate

Women Employed runs a free job problems counseling service through which they often receive complaints about sexual harassment. Women Employed also publishes a report entitled *Sexual Harassment in the Workplace*.

f. Women's Legal Defense Fund
    2000 P Street, N.W., Suite 400
    Washington, DC 20036

Phone: 202-986-2600

The Women's Legal Defense Fund works for women's rights in employment. The Fund has a special committee for counseling on employment discrimination, including discrimination in the form of harassment. Its publication is entitled *W.L.D.F. News* (quarterly). Call for more information about the Fund's publication, *Sexual Harassment in the Workplace*.

NOTES

1. The following texts will help non-lawyers doing legal research find their way around the library: N. JOHNSON, R. BERRING, AND T. WOXLAND, WINNING RESEARCH SKILLS (West Publishing Co., 1991); M. COHEN, R. BERRING, AND K. OLSON, HOW TO FIND THE LAW (West Publishing Co., 1989).

2. To talk to a LEXIS/NEXIS representative call (800) 543-6862 or write Mead Data Central, 9393 Springboro Pike, P.O. Box 933, Dayton, Ohio 45401.

3. To talk to a WESTLAW representative, call (800) 937-8529 or write West

Publishing Company, 50 W. Kellogg Blvd., P.O. Box 64526, St. Paul, MN 55164-0526.

4. For comparison of the information contained in these two services, see WESTLAW's *Database List* and LEXIS's *Library Contents and Alphabetical List*.

5. To get in touch with a LEXIS/NEXIS representative see note 2.

IV. Primary Sources

A. THE CASES

This section does not cite every case that involves a hostile environment claim. Instead, only the most current and most frequently mentioned federal supreme court and appellate court decisions are included. While some influential and interesting district court cases are cited, it is up to the researcher to look for cases in districts and on issues important to them. A sampling of EEOC decisions involving the hostile environment claim is also included below. Database and looseleaf services are among the best tools to use when looking for cases on the hostile environment claim. See Part III of this guide for more information on these and other research aids.

1. The Landmark Supreme Court Case–*Meritor Savings Bank v. Vinson*, 477 U.S. 57 (1986)

a. Judicial History

Ms. Vinson was initially denied relief by the district court. On appeal the court reversed and remanded the case due to the lower court's failure to consider both types of sexual harassment claims (quid pro quo and hostile environment). In doing so, the court of appeals held that, if a hostile environment existed, the Bank should be held strictly liable for the supervisor's conduct, despite its lack of knowledge.

b. Outcome

Meritor was the first case in which the United States Supreme Court recognized that sexual harassment based on a hostile environment claim is a violation of Title VII. In *Meri-*

tor, the court held that a hostile work environment existed where: (1) repeated demands for sexual favors from plaintiff's supervisor led to 40 or 50 acts of intercourse; (2) plaintiff's supervisor followed her into the restroom and exposed himself to her; and (3) plaintiff's supervisor forcibly raped her on several occasions. The court remanded Mechelle Vinson's case for consideration of her hostile environment claim.

c. Holdings

When Mechelle Vinson's case reached the United States Supreme Court, the Justices unanimously recognized sexual harassment as discrimination under Title VII and chose not to limit sexual harassment claims to those in which victims incurred a tangible loss. Although the Supreme Court required the plaintiff to establish that the conduct complained of was unwelcome, the court did not comment on what effect different allegations of welcomeness might have on the claim.

In addition, the Supreme Court held that the court of appeals erred in concluding that employers are always strictly liable for sexual harassment perpetrated by their employees. Instead, the court indicated that the issue of employer liability be resolved by reference to agency principles.

Finally, the Supreme Court held that the district court did not err in admitting evidence of the plaintiff's sexually provocative speech and dress, since it was relevant to the element of unwelcomeness. Because the Supreme Court left some issues open in *Meritor,* there is ongoing debate between legal scholars as to which standards should be adopted. Most of this debate centers on the issue of employer liability.

2. Court of Appeals Cases

a. *Andrews v. City of Philadelphia,* 895 F.2d 1469 (3rd Cir. 1990).

Here the district court held that the plaintiffs failed to prove a hostile environment because they did not complain to supervisors about the obscene language and pornographic pictures that allegedly offended them. In addition, the court found that many actions the plaintiffs complained of were not directed at the plaintiffs *because of their sex*. The court of appeals remanded the case to the district court, instructing the lower court to apply a *reasonable woman* standard.

b. *Chamberlain v. IOI Realty*, 915 F.2d 777 (1st Cir. 1990).

In this case the court held that when considering the welcomeness element of a hostile environment claim, the trier of fact must take into account that emphatic means of protesting unwelcome conduct may lead to retaliation. Where the plaintiff withdrew her hands from the defendant's hold, changed the subject when he initiated offensive conversation, and left his presence when other unwelcome conduct occurred, this element of her claim was satisfied.

c. *Downes v. Federal Aviation Admin.*, 775 F.2d 288 (Fed. Cir. 1985).

In *Downes* the Federal Circuit held that the context in which a gesture is made is a key factor in determining whether it will be considered offensive by a reasonable person. While the court acknowledged five occasions on which Mr. Downes harassed an employee, it held that the unwelcome conduct was not sufficiently severe to create a hostile working environment. According to the court, Mr. Downes testified that he merely touched his employee's hair in a friendly gesture while complimenting her on her new hair style.

d. *Drinkwater v. Union Carbide*, 904 F.2d 853 (3rd Cir. 1990).

Here the plaintiff advanced a hostile environment claim based on a relationship between a male supervisor and female co-employee. She alleged in her complaint that the relationship charged her work environment with sexual innuendo. While the court recognized that a hostile environment may be created from such a situation, it granted the defendant's motion for summary judgement because the plaintiff failed to demonstrate how the oppressive environment affected her ability to perform her work or her psychological well-being.

e. *Ellison v. Brady,* 924 F.2d 872 (9th Cir. 1991).

The Ninth Circuit reversed the district court's decision to grant the defendant's motion for summary judgement on the plaintiff's hostile environment claim. Instead, the court held that whether harassment was sufficiently severe and pervasive to constitute a hostile environment must be judged from the perspective of a reasonable woman. The court went on to hold that a reasonable woman would be affected by a co-worker who continually asks her out despite her rejections and who writes notes and letters confessing his obsession with her. The court also held that the employer's response to the plaintiff's complaint was not "reasonably calculated to end the harassment," since the employer transferred the harasser back to the plaintiff's office after her complaints and the harassment continued.

f. *Henson v. Dundee,* 682 F.2d 897 (11th Cir. 1982).

The court in *Henson* found that a hostile working environment existed where the chief of the police department made daily inquiries regarding his employee's sex life and used vulgar language when addressing her. The harassment was held sufficiently pervasive since the defendant also made repeated requests for sexual intercourse over a two-year period. In *Henson,* the Eleventh Circuit also lent meaning to the term "unwelcome" by defining unwelcome conduct as (1) conduct that the employee does not solicit or entice in any way, and (2) conduct that the employee regards as undesirable or offensive.

g. *Hicks v. Gates Rubber Co.,* 928 F.2d 966 (10th Cir. 1991).

In *Hicks,* the court of appeals affirmed the district court's decision that plaintiff Hicks did not prove hostile environment sexual harassment. Hicks alleged that her supervisor, Gleason, patted her on the butt and told her he would put his foot so far up it that she would have to go to a clinic to take it out. The court also considered evidence that Gleason called black people "niggers" and "coons," concluding that this evidence, while contributing to the totality of the circumstances in which her hostile environment claim must be considered, was not sufficiently severe and pervasive as required to state a claim.

h. *Jones v. Flagship Int'l*, 793 F.2d 714 (5th Cir. 1986).

In this case the court held that in the absence of tangible job detriment a plaintiff is required to make a commensurately stronger showing that the sexually harassing conduct was sufficiently pervasive. The court went on to hold that "distress" is not considered tangible job detriment. Although the plaintiff's employer propositioned her and made numerous other advances while they were traveling on business together, the court found that harassment was not sufficiently pervasive in her work environment to state a claim under Title VII.

i. *Jordan v. Clark*, 847 F.2d 1368 (9th Cir. 1988).

This case is of little use as precedent since the court does not explain in any detail the allegations of sexual harassment made by plaintiff. In addition, the court uses general language to explain its finding that the supervisor involved made sexist remarks to his female employee. The court goes on to conclude, however, that the plaintiff and her supervisor had been flirting with one another in a manner that is likely to have made both parties feel that they had been subjected to unwelcome advances. According to the court, "off-color jokes" and "misunderstood flirtatious conversations" are not enough to create a hostile working environment.

j. *King v. Board of Regents of the Univ. of Wisconsin*, 898 F.2d 533 (7th Cir. 1990).

Court of appeal in *King* affirmed the district court's finding of a hostile environment under Title VII when plaintiff was repeatedly verbally assaulted, fondled, and physically attacked. The plaintiff in this case had made clear to her harasser that his advances were unwelcome. The court used the reasonable person standard in determining that hostility in the environment was sufficiently severe and pervasive.

k. *Kotcher v. Rosa and Sullivan Appliance Center, Inc.*, 957 F.2d 59 (2nd Cir. 1992).

The district court in this case held that a supervisor's conduct toward his employee was sufficiently severe and pervasive to create an abusive working environment. Nevertheless, the lower court refused to hold the employer liable. On appeal, the Second Circuit held that the fact that the plaintiff had complained to co-employees and other supervisors about the defendant's conduct was not sufficient to give the employer constructive notice since their main office was in another town. The case was remanded for reconsideration of the unlawful retaliation issue.

l. *Rabidue v. Osceola Refining Co.*, 805 F.2d 611 (6th Cir. 1986).

In *Rabidue* the Sixth Circuit held that: (1) obscene comments made regularly by a male supervisor about women in general, (2) obscene comments made specifically about the plaintiff, and (3) posters of nude or scantily dressed women displayed in work areas were not so startling as to have affected seriously the psyche of the plaintiff or of other women employees. Since the supervisor's conduct failed to meet the sufficiently pervasive element of the claim, the court found that no hostile environment existed. A reasonable person standard was employed.

m. *Reed v. Shepard*, 939 F.2d 484 (7th Cir. 1991).

The trial court in *Reed* gave a directed verdict for the defendant in a hostile environment claim where the plaintiff alleged, among other things, that she was handcuffed to doors, had a cattle prod with an electric shock placed between her legs, and had her head forced into co-workers' laps. The district court did not credit the plaintiff's explanation for why it appeared that she actively participated in these antics. Her allegation that toleration of such behavior was necessary in order to keep her job was not good enough when other women who protested such treatment were successful in stopping its recurrence. The Seventh Circuit affirmed.

n. *Scott v. Sears Roebuck and Co.*, 798 F.2d 210 (7th Cir. 1986).

The court in *Scott* holds that even if each allegation of harassment in the plaintiff's complaint were proven, the incidents would fail to constitute behavior sufficiently severe to create an abusive working environment. It was not enough, according to the court, that the senior mechanic in the garage where Ms. Scott worked continually winked at her, asked to give her a rubdown, and slapped her behind. In addition, Ms. Scott alleged that he withheld work-related advice from her, asking what he would get in exchange for the information.

o. *Vinson v. Taylor*, 735 F.2d 141 (D.C. Cir. 1985).

This case addresses the issue of whether a plaintiff who is not the object of harassment, but who works in an environment where another person is being harassed, can bring a hostile environment claim under Title VII. In dicta, the court held that such a claim is possible when hostility so permeates the plaintiff's environment that it becomes a condition of her employment.

p. *Wilson v. Zapata Off-Shore Co.*, 939 F.2d 260 (5th Cir. 1991).

The defendant's verdict in hostile environment case is affirmed in *Wilson* on the grounds that even though the plaintiff testified to conduct that constitutes sexual harassment, the trier of fact is free to disbelieve her testimony in light of contradictory evidence given by defendant. Since no clear error was found, the verdict was affirmed.

q. *Wyerick v. Bayou Steel Corp.*, 887 F.2d 1271 (5th Cir. 1989).

The court of appeal reversed the lower court's decision to grant summary judgment to the employer in a sexual harassment case. According to the Fifth Circuit, the plaintiff's three sexual comments made in response to an "onslaught" of sexual remarks and conduct by the defendant does not preclude her opportunity to demonstrate that his remarks were unwelcome.

r. *Yates v. Avco, Corp.,* 819 F.2d 630 (6th Cir. 1987).

The court in *Yates* determined that a supervisor's harassing conduct was within the scope of his employment. Where management investigated the complaints and put the supervisor on administrative leave, but then asked employees not to go to the EEOC with their complaints, refused to alter documents to indicate that employee absence was due to harassment, and failed to provide employees with copies of their stated complaints, the employer may be held liable.

3. District Court Cases

a. *Ambrose v. United States Steel Corp.,* 39 FEP Cases 30 (N. Dist. C.A. 1985).

In this case a female guard claimed that she was sexually harassed by her supervisor. The court found that a supervisor's flirtatious overtures, attempts to kiss the plaintiff, and inquiry into her experiences with oral sex were enough to create a hostile working environment that negatively affected the plaintiff's psyche. In addition, the court held that evidence of the supervisor's harassment of other women is relevant to demonstrating that the hostility was sufficiently pervasive. When faced with the task of adopting a standard of employer liability, the court chose to follow the D.C. Circuit in *Vinson,* 743 F.2d 141, rather than the Eleventh Circuit in *Henson,* 682 F.2d 897, and held the employer strictly liable for incidents of harassment, regardless of the employer's actual or constructive knowledge.

b. *Broderick v. Ruder,* 685 F.Supp. 1269 (D.C.C. 1988).

The court considered evidence of general work atmosphere to determine whether the plaintiff, who was not herself the subject of harassment, had a valid claim. Because the plaintiff was unmotivated and discouraged as a result of working in an environment where managers gave preferential treatment to those who complied with sexual requests, the court found a Title VII violation.

c. *Campbell v. Kansas State Univ.*, 780 F.Supp. 755 (D. Kan. 1991).

In this case the district court found the plaintiff's hostile environment claim meritorious. It found the defendant university liable for the supervisor's actions on two separate grounds: (1) employer negligence and recklessness and (2) inclusion of the perpetrator in a broadly defined notion of employer, so that agency principles were not even at issue.

d. *Cook v. Yellow Freight System, Inc.*, 53 FEP Cases 1681 (E. Dist. C.A. 1990).

In *Cook* the district court for the Eastern District of California allowed the plaintiff to discover the names of the employees who previously worked with her supervisor. Discovery was allowed only for the purpose of sending these women a letter, approved by the court, about her pending hostile environment claim. The court denied permission, however, for the plaintiff to discover documentation of a settlement discussion she had with her employer, due to overriding privacy concerns. Plaintiff sought the information to establish her claim that numerous incidents of sexual harassment by her supervisor had created a hostile working environment in violation of Title VII.

e. *Hansel v. Pub. Service Co. of Colorado*, 778 F.Supp 1126 (D. Colo. 1991).

The district court in *Hansel* found sufficient evidence to conclude that the plaintiff was subjected to a hostile environment at work when, among other things, her breasts and genitals were fondled. The court went on to hold that even though the physical harassment had stopped, the employer's response of "discussing the matter" with the perpetrators was not reasonably calculated to diffuse the hostile environment.

f. *Jenson v. Eveleth Taconite Co.*, 57 FEP Cases 867 (Minn. 5th Div. 1991).

The court heard evidence regarding sexually explicit graffiti and posters in common areas, unwelcome touching, and comments from men that women do not belong in mines but belong at home with their children. Based on this evidence the court found that a sufficiently defined class existed as to the plaintiffs' hostile environment sexual harassment class action claim.

g. *Priest v. Rotary*, 634 F.Supp. 571 (N. Dist. C.A. 1986).

The court in *Priest* found that the incidents complained of were neither isolated nor trivial and were sufficiently pervasive to alter the plaintiff's working conditions and create a hostile working environment. The plaintiff was awarded back pay. Unlawful conduct by the coffee shop supervisor that was alleged and established by the plaintiff included, but was not limited to: (1) putting his arms around her from the back, (2) putting his hands on her breasts, (3) kissing her neck, (4) trapping her between himself and another male employee while rubbing up against her, (5) exposing his genitals to her, and (6) fondling other waitresses in her presence.

h. *Robinson v. Jacksonville Shipyards*, 760 F.Supp. 1486 (M.D. F.L., 1991).

The court awarded injunctive relief to the plaintiff, who is a female, African-American ship-welder. Robinson complained of pornographic pin-ups throughout her workplace and lewd remarks from co-workers. After protesting to management, the comments increased and a "Men Only" sign was hung on the door to an area where pornography was located. The court concluded that a reasonable woman would find that such behavior creates a hostile and offensive working environment in violation of Title VII.

4. Equal Employment Opportunity Commission Decisions

a. EEOC D. No. 86-6, 40 FEP Cases 1890 (Jan. 24, 1986).

The Commission found that the plaintiff was subjected to sexual harassment at work, but did not hold the employer liable, since they discharged the harasser following her complaint.

b. EEOC D. No. 85-9, 37 FEP Cases 1893 (June 11th, 1985).

Despite the fact that the charging parties in this case never actually wore swimwear to work, the EEOC found that requiring them to do so might still be a violation of Title VII of the Civil Rights Act of 1964. In answering the question "Is the conduct based on sex?" the court looked at the totality of the circumstances to see whether two factors were met. First, the EEOC found that the required outfit was "revealing." The second prong of the EEOC's "based on sex" test, however, requires that wearing the outfit was likely to result in unwelcome sexual harassment which would create a hostile working environment. Employing this reasoning, the EEOC found that it was unlikely such harassment would result and thus found no violation of Title VII.

c. EEOC D. No. 84-3, 34 FEP Cases 1887 (Feb. 16, 1984).

Here the Commission found that a hostile environment was created when a group of men came into the restaurant where charging party worked and grabbed her butt underneath her skirt stating that they were only placing their orders. The waitress complained to her manager who failed to take prompt and effective remedial action. Instead, the manager, who was a friend of the harassers, went out drinking with them after their meal. The Commission held the employer liable.

d. EEOC D. 84-1, 33 FEP Cases 1887 (Nov. 28, 1983).

The Commission found that a hostile environment was created (as to charging parties A and C) by their employer's daily comments about sex. It also found that charging party B's participation in jokes of a sexual nature contradicted her allegation that the conduct was unwelcome. The Commission held that as a general rule charging parties who have participated in such behavior must affirmatively indicate that it is no longer welcome. B did not meet this requirement.

e. EEOC D. 83-1, 31 FEP Cases 1852 (Oct. 7, 1982).

In this decision, the Commission found that a hostile environment was created when a co-worker forcibly kissed the plaintiff at work and later confronted her to ask who she had told. Commission did not, however, hold the employer liable for the acts, since prompt and effective remedial action was taken upon the charging party's complaint. Investigation was completed within a week, the harasser was demoted, given a salary cut, and warned that future conduct would result in further disciplinary action.

f. EEOC D. No. 81-23, 27 FEP Cases 1816 (June 3rd, 1981).

The EEOC held that only one instance of sexual harassment, where the charging party's supervisor indicated that he wanted her all to himself, is not sufficient to demonstrate an offensive environment or to establish interference with the charging party's work performance. The EEOC found no wrongful termination, since many reasons existed for her termination, other than her refusal of the supervisor's come-on. In reaching the conclusion that Title VII was not violated, the EEOC stressed the fact that no one else had complained of harassment, and the charging party's allegation was uncorroborated.

g. EEOC D. No. 81-18, 27 FEP Cases 1793 (April 3rd, 1981).

Five charging parties employed at a rehabilitation camp for boys brought hostile environment claims against their supervisor. The EEOC recognized in this case that dinner and lunch invitations can be counted as instances of harassment when the defendant makes clear that he is seeking the women's company because he is "hot for them."

In holding that harassment was sufficiently pervasive, the EEOC found the following conduct to have occurred: (1) the supervisor used vulgar and sexually explicit language when addressing the charging parties, (2) the supervisor attempted to cuddle, kiss, hug, and touch the employees, and also attempted to pin one woman against the wall, (3) the supervisor constantly extended dinner and lunch invitations to the charging parties, (4) the supervisor commented to one employee that her hair looked like a sheep's and that she better stay away from any herds unless she wanted to get "rammed."

h. EEOC D. No. 81-17, 27 FEP Cases 1791 (Feb. 6th, 1981).

According to the EEOC, a charging party can bring a hostile environment claim when her supervisor makes sexual demands of her and requires her to wear a revealing costume.

B. FEDERAL STATUTE

Hostile environment sexual harassment is actionable as sex discrimination under Title VII of the Civil Rights Act of 1964, as amended, §§2000e et seq. While the *United States Code* is cited below, the annotated codes will also provide listings of cases that interpret the statutory language. Either *United States Code Service* or *United States Annotated* are good for this purpose. Below are a few of Title VII's important subsections.

1. 42 U.S.C. §2000e. Definitions

   Defines terms such as "employer," "employee," and "on the basis of sex" for the purposes of 42 U.S.C. §§2000e et seq.

2. 42 U.S.C. §2000e-2. Unlawful Employment Practices

   §2000e-2(a)(1) defines unlawful employer practices. It states: "It shall be an unlawful employment practice for an employer to fail or refuse to hire or to discharge any individual, or otherwise to discriminate against any individual with respect to compensation, terms, conditions, or privileges of employment, because of such individual's race, color, religion, sex, or national origin."

3. 42 U.S.C. §2000e-4. Equal Employment Opportunity Commission

   This section creates the EEOC and describes its function. Subsection 2000e-4(g) specifically gives the Commission power to furnish technical assistance to persons subject to §2000e et seq. and to make technical studies appropriate to effectuate the purposes and policies of Title VII.

4. 42 U.S.C. §2000e-5. Enforcement Provisions

Section 2000e-5(a) empowers the Commission to "prevent any person from engaging in any unlawful employment practice as set forth in [42 U.S.C. §§2000e-2 or 2000e-3]." Section 2000e-5 also provides procedural instructions on commencement of proceedings, time for filing charges, and notice. The availability of injunctions, reinstatement, back pay, and other equitable relief for violation of this title is outlined in §2000e-5(g).

5. 42 U.S.C. § 1981a.

This code section sets forth the limited amount of compensatory and punitive damages available to victims of unlawful, intentional discrimination as defined in Section 2000e-2.

C. FEDERAL REGULATION

The EEOC's "Guidelines on Discrimination Because of Sex" are found in 29 C.F.R. Part 1604. This part is indexed under the term "sexual harassment." Use C.F.R.'s *List of Sections Affected* for updating. 29 C.F.R. §1604.11 states that harassment on the basis of sex is a violation of Title VII when such conduct has the "purpose or effect of unreasonably interfering with an individual's work performance or creating an intimidating, hostile, or offensive working environment."

V. Secondary Sources

Chances are that researchers interested in hostile environment sexual harassment will not learn all they need to know about the claim from reading Title VII and the court decisions on point. Instead, researchers may need to consult secondary sources of information to supplement their understanding of the law. The resources described below include a wide variety of information so that victims, employers, practitioners, and scholars will all find this section useful in attaining an understanding of the hostile environment claim suited to their needs. Included in this section is an analysis of annotations, bibliographies, books, briefs, employer tools, EEOC guidelines, journal and law review articles, legal encyclopedias, newspaper and magazine articles, practitioner tools, statistical surveys, textbooks, treatises, and videos that are relevant to the hostile environment claim.

A. ANNOTATIONS

Annotations lay out the law in a straightforward format and provide valuable references to other sources such as cases, statutes, law review articles, and encyclopedias. To locate annotations on the hostile environment claim, look up "Sexual Discrimination" in A.L.R.'s *Index to Annotations* or do a full-text search on LEXIS in ALR. ANNO[1] The subtopic "Harassment–Sexual" refers you to annotations on point. Since annotations are supplemented annually, they are also useful as a quick reference for up-to-date law.

1. Right on Point–Must See

When Is Work Environment Intimidating, Hostile, or Offensive, so as to Constitute Sexual Harassment in Violation of Title

VII of Civil Rights Act of 1964, as Amended (42 U.S.C.S. §§2000e et seq.), 78 A.L.R. Fed. 252 (Lawyers Co-op. Pub. Co., 1989).

2. Broader in Scope–Also Good

a. *Construction and Application of Provisions of Title VII of Civil Rights Act of 1964 (42 U.S.C.S. §§2000e et seq.) Making Sex Discrimination in Employment Unlawful,* 12 A.L.R. Fed. 15 (Lawyers Co-op. Pub. Co., 1989).

b. *Discoverability and Admissibility of Plaintiff's Past Sexual Behavior in Title VII Sexual Harassment Action,* 73 A.L.R. Fed. 748 (Lawyers Co-op Pub. Co., 1989).

c. *Liability Under Title VII of Civil Rights Act of 1964 (42 U.S.C.S. §§2000e et seq.) of Employer, as Successor Employer, for Discriminatory Employment Practices of Predecessor,* 67 A.L.R. Fed. 806 (Lawyers Co-op. Pub. Co., 1984).

d. *On-the-Job Sexual Harassment as a Violation of State Civil Rights Law,* 18 A.L.R. 4th 328 (Lawyers Co-op. Pub. Co., 1982).

e. *Sexual Advances by Employee's Superior as Sex Discrimination Within Title VII of Civil Rights Act of 1964 (42 U.S.C.S. §§2000e et seq.),* 46 A.L.R. Fed. 224 (Lawyers Co-op. Pub. Co., 1989).

3. Title VII Remedies

a. *Award of Attorneys' Fees Under §706(k) of Civil Rights Act of 1964 (42 U.S.C.S. §§2000e-5(k)) Authorizing Court to Allow Prevailing Party, Other Than Equal Employment Opportunity Commission or United States, Reasonable Attorney's Fee as Part of Costs in Action Under Equal Employment Opportunities Part of Act,* 16 A.L.R. Fed. 643 (Lawyers Co-op. Pub. Co., 1989).

b. *Award of Back Pay in Suit Under Title VII of Civil Rights Act of 1964 (42 U.S.C.S. §§2000e et seq.), for Discriminatory Employment Practices*, 21 A.L.R. Fed. 472 (Lawyers Co-op. Pub. Co., 1989).

c. *Award of Compensatory Damages, Aside From Backpay or Frontpay, for Violation of Title VII of Civil Rights Act of 1964 (42 U.S.C.S. §§2000e et seq.)*, 48 A.L.R. Fed 338 (Lawyers Co-op. Pub. Co., 1989).

B. BIBLIOGRAPHIES

The best bibliographies on sexual harassment are listed below. All are well-annotated and provide great leads. For those interested specifically in the hostile environment claim, however, there are faster ways to get to the relevant material.

1. NOW LEGAL DEFENSE AND EDUCATION FUND. SELECTED, ANNOTATED BIBLIOGRAPHY ON SEXUAL HARASSMENT (1990).

   Outstanding bibliography which includes references to books, reports, legal and general articles, pamphlets, charts, packages, and training resources for employers. For information on how to order, call NOW Legal Defense and Education Fund at (212) 925-6635.

2. MCCAGHY, SEXUAL HARASSMENT, A GUIDE TO RESOURCES (G.K. Hall & Co., 1985).

3. Wallentine, *Sex for Success: A Pathfinder for Sexual Harassment Actions*. LEGAL REFERENCE SERVICES QUARTERLY, VOL. 10(4) 1990. (The Haworth Press, Inc., 1991).

C. BOOKS

There are not many books that focus on hostile environment as a legal claim. Most of the publications listed below deal with sexual harassment generally and only make short mention of the hostile environment claim. In addition, books that focus on the legal claim become quickly outdated. To look for new publications use the card catalogue or computerized system at any public library. Books on sexual harassment are usually categorized under headings such as "Sexual Harassment," "Women and Employment," or "Employment Discrimination." Libraries that specialize in women's issues are likely to have more relevant publications available.[2]

1. Best Books

a. GUTEK, SEX AND THE WORKPLACE: THE IMPACT OF SEXUAL BEHAVIOR AND HARASSMENT ON WOMEN, MEN AND ORGANIZATIONS. (Jossey-Bass Publishers, 1985).

Examines the attitudes of men and women about sexuality in the workplace. Author describes the results of her study on the characteristics of harassers and reactions of victims.

b. MACKINNON, SEXUAL HARASSMENT OF WORKING WOMEN, A CASE OF SEX DISCRIMINATION. (Yale University Press, 1979).

Catharine MacKinnon is an expert in the field of sexual harassment law. Her book provides a thought-provoking analysis of the problem of sexual harassment of working women. MacKinnon explains how her dominance approach to gender theory plays out in the area of sexual harassment. Her critique of sexual harassment law in its early stages is still relevant since many issues she examines have yet to be resolved.

c. OMILIAN, SEXUAL HARASSMENT IN EMPLOYMENT. (Callaghan & Company, 1987).

Straightforward presentation of the legal and practical issues of sexual harassment at work. Especially valuable for its sections on special litigation issues, alternative legal claims, and legal issues yet to be resolved.

2. Other Books

a. MASCHKE, LITIGATION, COURTS AND WOMEN WORKERS. (Praeger Publishers, 1989).

b. MEYER, BERCHTOLD, OESTREICH & COLLINS, SEXUAL HA-RASSMENT. (Petrocelli Books, 1981).

c. PEPPER, KENNEDY, SEX DISCRIMINATION IN EMPLOYMENT. (The Michie Company, 1981).

D. BRIEFS

While not of primary importance in your research of the claim, the briefs filed on behalf of the petitioner and respondent in *Meritor Savings Bank v. Vinson*[3] are interesting to look at. Arguments made by both sides in *Meritor* are not moot considering the unsettled state of many hostile environment issues, including employer liability, discoverable evidence, and the reasonable person standard. Of the 14 briefs filed in this case the four to look at are cited below.

1. Brief for The United States and The Equal Employment Opportunity Commission as Amici Curiae. *Meritor Savings Bank, FSB, Petitioner v. Mechelle Vinson*, No. 84-1979, October Term, 1985, December, 11, 1985.

2. Brief of Respondent, Mechelle Vinson. *Meritor Savings Bank, FSB, Petitioner v. Mechelle Vinson*, No. 84-1979, October Term, 1985, February, 11, 1986.

3. Brief of Working Women's Institute as Amici Curiae in Support of Respondent. *Meritor Savings Bank, FSB, Petitioner v. Mechelle Vinson*, No. 84-1979, October Term.

4. Brief of Petitioner, Meritor Savings Bank, FSB. *Meritor Savings Bank, FSB, Petitioner v. Mechelle Vinson*, No. 84-1979, October Term, 1985, December 11, 1985.

E. EMPLOYER TOOLS

Employers concerned about the threat of liability for sexual harassment should find much of the information contained in this guide useful when creating a plan to maintain a workplace free from harassment. The resources listed below, however, particularly concern the issue of prevention.

1. Publications

a. BAXTER, SEXUAL HARASSMENT IN THE WORKPLACE: A GUIDE TO THE LAW. (Executive Enterprises Pub. Co., Inc., 1981).

Very practical guide to the law addressed to employers. Includes hypothetical examples of sexual harassment at work and proper employer responses.

b. MCQUEEN, THE MANAGEMENT VIEW: SEXUAL HARASSMENT IN THE WORKPLACE. (McQueen & Son Publishing Co., 1982).

Provides answers to questions frequently asked by employers. Includes reviews of educational movies for management as well as sample grievance forms. Describes appropriate management policies against harassment and methods of processing complaints.

c. WOLDT, SEXUAL HARASSMENT IN THE WORKPLACE, A PRACTICAL GUIDE FOR EMPLOYERS. (California Continuing Education of the Bar, 1992).

Excellent resource for employers. This softbound handbook is written specifically for employers to understand and benefit from. The author describes policies and procedures that employers can adopt to alleviate the problem of sexual harassment at work. She provides model language for personnel manuals and workshops, proposes internal procedures for handling grievances, and more–all designed to minimize employers' exposure to sexual harassment claims.

2. Videos

a. *Preventing Sexual Harassment*
BNA Communications
1750 Montgomery Street
San Francisco, CA 94111

A BNA Communications training aide for employers. Depicts the negative effects of harassment on the work environment. 20 minutes.

b. *Sexual Harassment: Walking the Corporate Fine Line*
   NOW Legal Defense & Education Fund
   99 Hudson Street
   New York, NY 10013

   Explains the legal definition of sexual harassment set out by the Supreme Court in *Meritor Savings Bank v. Vinson.* Outlines the basics of developing an effective sexual harassment policy.

c. *Workplace Hustle*
   Clark Communications, Inc.
   943 Howard Street
   San Francisco, CA 94103
   415-777-1668

   This 32-minute film is designed to inform and sensitize the viewer to the damaging effects of sexual harassment. Also provides commentary on how to prevent harassment from occurring.

F. EEOC POLICY GUIDANCE MANUAL

EEOC Policy Guidance on Current Issues of Sexual Harassment is a procedural handbook that was issued by the Commission to its field office personnel in 1990. The manual spells out in greater detail how the EEOC feels its regulations prohibiting sexual harassment at work should be interpreted.[4] In addition, the manual provides guidance on how to determine when hostile environment sexual harassment has occurred and how to establish employer liability in light of recent cases. Courts seem to pay close attention to the EEOC's position in regard to sexual harassment at work, so this manual is a valuable resource. Be sure to look for the most recent version.[5]

G. JOURNAL ARTICLES

There have not been many journal articles written specifically on the subject of hostile environment sexual harassment. Instead, law review articles are the best source of periodical literature for information on the claim. Listed below are a few journal articles worth reading. For information on how to find journal articles using database services or indexes to periodical literature, see Part III.

1. John S. Moot, comment, *An Analysis of Judicial Deference to the EEOC Interpretive Guidelines*, 1 ADMIN. L. J. 213 (Summer, 1987).

   Author recognizes that there are two models applied to the construction of sexual harassment under Title VII. He calls them the Independent Judgement and Deferential models. He argues that, since the plain language of Title VII is ambiguous as to sexual harassment claims, the courts should defer to the EEOC Guidelines where they are reasonable and consistent. The author also calls for strict employer liability.

2. Cynthia F. Cohen, article, *Legal Dilemmas in Sexual Harassment Cases*, 38 LAB. L. J. 681 (November, 1987).

   Author hopes the EEOC will attempt to eliminate ambiguities in the law. Article covers issues including employer liability, admissible testimony, forms of relief, employee actions, and future public policy.

3. Hope A. Comisky, article, *"Prompt and Effective Remedial Action?" What Must an Employer Do to Avoid Liability for "Hostile Work Environment" Sexual Harassment?*, 8 LAB. LAW, 181 (Spring, 1992).

   The meanings of "effective" policy against sexual harassment and "prompt" and "effective" investigation of charges are defined by providing specific examples of scenarios that are likely to be sufficient and insufficient to a court. In addition, author describes how monitoring can be accomplished in a useful manner and when termination is a necessary step in avoiding liability.

4. *Psychiatric Injury in the Women's Workplace*, 13 BULL. AM. ACAD. PSYCHIATRY L. 399 (1985).

Short article, but good in that it addresses the problem of compliance. Describes psychological reactions to sexual harassment which may explain why women often comply with such behavior, despite the fact that it is unwelcome. Uses three hypotheticals to illustrate possible reactions to harassment.

5. Charles S. Mishkind, article, *Sexual Harassment Hostile Work Environment Class Actions: Is There a Cause for Concern?*, 18 EMPLOYEE REL. L. J. 141 (Summer, 1992).

Author feels that innovative plaintiff's attorneys will include sexual harassment claims in "across the board" class actions for leverage in settlement negotiations. Effective preventative measures against sexual harassment are suggested as the best way to address the increased risk to employers in this area.

6. William A. Nowlin, article, *Sexual Harassment in the Workplace: How Arbitrators Rule*, 43 ARB. J. 31 (December, 1988).

Great article addressing the regulatory framework which governs sexual harassment. Examines both cases brought by victims as well as "just-cause" cases brought by alleged offenders. Author explains that most sexual harassment cases that arrive in arbitration are actually just-cause cases brought by employees disciplined by management in response to internal sexual harassment complaints.

7. Edward J. Costello, Jr., article, *The Mediation Alternative in Sex Harassment Cases*, 47 ARB. J. 16 (March, 1992).

Author explains reasons why mediation in sexual harassment cases is a favorable alternative to litigation. He concludes that in most cases all those involved save time and money through mediation. In addition, author suggests that the results are more frequently fair and just when compared to the results of litigation.

H. LAW REVIEW ARTICLES

Compared to all the other resources outlined in this guide, law review articles provide the current and thorough legal analysis of the hostile environment claim. Most of the notes and comments listed below also trace the development of the claim and of sexual harassment law in general. Law review articles are especially valuable for those who are interested in a critical analysis of the claim. These articles will also lead you to cases on point.

There are hundreds of articles written on sexual harassment in the workplace, many of which include discussion of the hostile environment claim. The articles, notes, and comments listed below were selected because they provide the best and most current analysis on a variety of issues central to the hostile environment claim. Some are lengthy, in-depth articles, some are concise overviews, but all are well-written and well-researched. Also noted below are articles that, while current and seemingly on point, are not worth your time.

Researchers looking for a particular kind of article can decide for themselves which ones will best suit their information needs by reading the descriptions that follow. For help on how to find law review articles using the database services or indexes to legal periodicals, see Part III.

1. The Hostile Environment Claim Generally

a. Christopher P. Barton, note, *Between the Boss and a Hard Place: A Consideration of Meritor Savings Bank, FSB v. Vinson and the Law of Sexual Harassment,* 67 B. U. L. REV. 45 (May, 1987).

   Intelligent discussion of the social and legal issues surrounding sexual harassment at work. Considers in depth the two issues left unresolved by the Supreme Court in *Meritor:* employer liability and unwelcomeness. Also provides a full picture of the legal and legislative history of the hostile environment claim.

b. Barbara L. Zalucki, comment, *Discrimination Law–Defining Hostile Environment,* 11 W. NEW ENG. L. REV. 143 (1989).

Summarizes the development of the sexual harassment claim focusing on the importance of the EEOC Guidelines. Provides examples of fact patterns that clearly constitute claims, and fact patterns that produce controversy. Author recognizes that behavior directed towards a woman because of her gender rather than because of sexual interest, is not always defined as a violation by the courts.

c. Becky Leamon, article, *Employers' Liability for Failure to Prevent Sexual Harassment*, 55 Mo. L. Rev. 803 (Summer, 1990).

Short note that merely describes facts of the case and legal reasoning used by the Fourth Circuit in *Paroline v. Unisys Corp*, 879 F.2d 100 (4th Cir. 1989).

d. Joshua F. Thorpe, note, *Gender-Based Harassment and the Hostile Work Environment*, 1990 Duke L. J. 1361 (December, 1990).

Part III of this article is of particular interest. In this part, the author compares court decisions that do not recognize non-sexual harassment as violative of Title VII to decisions that recognize gender discrimination as actionable under Title VII, regardless of whether it was sexually motivated. Author concludes that the latter class of cases, though ambiguous in their reasoning, are correct on this issue.

e. Jill W. Henken, note, *Hostile Environment Claims of Sexual Harassment: The Continuing Expansion of Sexual Harassment Law*, 34 Vill. L. Rev. 1243 (1989).

Recognizes that with the adoption of the hostile environment claim, sexual harassment claims are an option for women who are not themselves the object of harassment. Looks at the first cases to make this breakthrough. Argues that a reasonable victim standard should be adopted.

f. Martha Sperry, comment, *Hostile Environment Sexual Harassment and the Imposition of Liability Without Notice: A Progressive Approach to Traditional Gender Roles and Power Based Relationships*, 24 New Eng. L. Rev. 917 (Spring, 1990).

Comment primarily looks at Massachusetts state anti-discrimination law. Argues that the court in *College-Town, Division of Interco, Inc. v. Massachusetts Commission Against Discrimination*, 508 N.E.2d 587 (1987) was correct in adopting the same standard of liability for supervisors in quid pro quo and hostile environment cases.

g. Nancy Braun, note, *Meritor Savings Bank v. Vinson: Clarifying the Standards of Hostile Working Environment Sexual Harassment*, 25 Hous. L. Rev. 441 (March, 1988).

Not the most comprehensive review of the *Meritor* decision. Author praises the decision for providing incentives to employers and reassurance to women. In Part V she suggests strategies for avoiding liability in sexual harassment claims.

h. M. Jule Courtney, note, *Meritor Savings Bank v. Vinson: Finally a Supreme Court Ruling on Sexual Harassment in the Workplace: For What It's Worth*, 38 Mercer L. Rev. 733 (Winter, 1987).

Provides a brief overview of the history of the hostile environment claim, as well as a concise summary of the *Meritor* decision. Argues that the Supreme Court in *Meritor* should have adopted a standard of strict employer liability for the discriminatory acts of supervisors and agents, regardless of employer knowledge.

i. Grace M. Dodier, case comment, *Meritor Savings Bank v. Vinson: Sexual Harassment at Work*, 10 Harv. Women's L. J. 203 (Spring, 1987).

Valuable as a straightforward analysis of *Meritor*. Highlights the important legal issues without getting bogged down in analytical critique.

j. Suzanne Egan, note, *Meritor Savings Bank v. Vinson: Title VII Liability for Sexual Harassment*, 17 Golden Gate U. L. Rev. 379 (Fall, 1987).

Includes a good review of the historical cases leading to the development of the hostile environment claim and the important cases pre-*Meritor*. Also offers a detailed critique of *Meritor*. Especially helpful because the author addresses the *unwelcomeness* issue, focusing on whether evidence of the victim's style of dress and past sexual behavior should be admitted.

k. Shannon Murphy, case note, *Meritor Savings Bank v. Vinson: What Makes a Work Environment "Hostile"?* 40 ARK. L. REV. 857.

Well-written and organized case note. Author does not purport to do anything more that explain the holding. Great for those who want a straightforward analysis of the case.

l. Karen Ervin Dooley, case comment, *Sexual Harassment–Highlander v. K.F.C. National Management Co.: Quid Pro Quo and Hostile Working Environment Distinctions*, 18 MEM. ST. U.L. REV. 183 (Fall, 1987).

Short comment that points out the overlap between the hostile environment and quid pro quo claims in certain situations. Expresses frustration at the courts' refusal to recognize that a hostile working environment is likely to result in denial of an employment benefit, constituting quid pro quo harassment, and that quid pro quo harassment often creates a hostile environment.

m. Marlissa Vinciguerra, note, *The Aftermath of Meritor: A Search for Standards in the Law of Sexual Harassment*, 98 YALE L. J. 1717 (June, 1989).

Author uses *Meritor* as a backdrop for examining the erosion of the quid pro quo claim caused by the adoption of a hostile environment claim. Traces the history of both claims. Concludes that overextension of the hostile environment claim is dangerous because the relief it provides is not as complete as the relief provided by a quid pro quo claim.

n. Lisa Rhode, case note, *The Sixth Circuit's Double Standard in Hostile Work Environment Claims: Davis v. Monsanto Chemical Co., 858 F.2d 345 (6th Cir. 1988)*, 58 U. CIN. L. REV. 779 (1989).

Reviews the Sixth Circuit's treatment of sex and race discrimination cases. Recognizes that flirting can serve a legitimate social function, where racial epithets cannot. Still concludes that it is unfair for victims of sexual harassment to be held to a higher standard of proof.

2. Standing

a. N. Morrison Torrey, article, *Indirect Discrimination Under Title VII: Expanding Male Standing to Sue for Injuries Received as a Result of Employer Discrimination Against Females,* 64 WASH. L. REV. 365 (April, 1989).

Criticizes the Ninth Circuit for refusing to give men standing to sue when they have been injured by the sexual harassment of women. Author concludes that this restrictive reading is inconsistent with Title VII's purpose and with traditional standing principles.

b. David Holtzman and Eric Trelz, article, *Recent Developments in the Law of Sexual Harassment: Abusive Environment Claims After Meritor Savings Bank v. Vinson,* 31 ST. LOUIS U. L. J. 239 (March 1987).

Long but thorough discussion of the important federal and Missouri cases, including an insightful evaluation of *Meritor.* Focuses on the issue of standing. Author argues that liberal rules of standing and liability are important because state laws do not always provide legal theories sufficient to hold perpetrators responsible.

3. Reasonable Person Standard

a. P. J. Murray, comment, *Employer Beware of Hostile Environment,* 26 DUQ. L. REV. 461 (Winter, 1988).

Author argues that claim should be evaluated using the "reasonable person in same or similar circumstances" standard. Feels that viewing the situation subjectively, through the eyes of the victim, would flood the courts with hostile environment claims. Comment is written for employers and serves primarily as a guide for avoiding liability.

b. Sheryl Hahn, note, *Evolution of the Hostile Workplace Claim Under Title VII: Only Sensitive Men Need Apply*, 22 GOLDEN GATE U. L. REV. 69 (Spring, 1992).

Straightforward review of *Ellison* case. Author praises Ninth Circuit for adopting the reasonable woman standard.

c. Cheryl L. Dragel, note, *Hostile Environment Sexual Harassment: Should the Ninth Circuit's "Reasonable Woman" Standard be Adopted?* 11 J. L. & COM. 237 (Spring, 1992).

Interesting review of reasonable woman standard set forth in *Ellison*. Author expresses doubt that gendered standard is the best way to address the problem since it removes women's experiences to a "separate sphere" reinforcing the notion of difference. As an alternative, author suggests exploring the assumption underlying the traditional reasonable person standard and calls for a more inclusive rethinking of personhood.

d. Nancy S. Ehrenreich, article, *Pluralist Myths and Powerless Men: Ideology of Reasonableness in Sexual Harassment Law*, 99 YALE L. J. 1177 (April, 1990).

Asks the question, "Why, despite recent scholarship revealing that judicial definitions of reasonableness often reflect the value and assumptions of a narrow elite, is the 'objective test' seen as an accurate reflection of societal norms at all?" Argues that hostile environment claims should be evaluated by a reasonable woman standard. Pays attention to the social dynamics that shape the legal claim.

e. Bonnie B. Westman, note, *The Reasonable Woman Standard: Preventing Sexual Harassment in the Workplace*, 18 WM. MITCHELL L. REV. 795 (Summer, 1992).

In-depth look at issues surrounding the reasonable woman standard. Author concludes that the Eighth Circuit should adopt this test. According to author, a standard that treats men and women the same begs the question: "The same as whom?"

f. David I. Gedrose, note, *Workplace Sexual Harassment: The Ninth Circuit's Reasonable Woman Standard and Employer Remedial Actions in Hostile Environment Claims Following Ellison v. Brady,* 28 WILLIAMETTE L. REV. 151 (Winter, 1991)

Note analyzes recent Ninth Circuit case that adopted reasonable woman standard in hostile environment sexual harassment cases. Also pays attention to other issues brought to light in *Ellison*, including harasser's continued presence in the workplace, male fact finder's ability to evaluate harassment claims, and distinguishing between reasonable and hyper-sensitive plaintiffs.

4. Welcomeness Issue

a. Susan R. Estrich, article, *Sex at Work*, 43 STAN. L. REV. 813 (April, 1991).

According to the author, the welcomeness inquiry should be eliminated from the hostile environment claim, because its additional requirements of proof are unnecessary from a doctrinal standpoint and it is personally humiliating for plaintiffs. She compares the unwelcomeness requirement to the consent standard in rape law and argues that the standard allows courts to conclude that plaintiffs who dress fashionably or keep quiet "asked for it."

b. Mary Jo Shaney, note, *Perceptions of Harm: The Consent Defense in Sexual Harassment Cases*, 71 IOWA L. REV. 1109 (May, 1986).

Although this note was written before *Meritor*, it proposes adoption of a consent standard that may still be relevant, especially considering the Supreme Court's failure to specify a standard to be used in establishing that harassment is unwelcome. The author suggests that a definition of valid consent should rest on overt indications of consent freely given, and that silent acquiescence be deemed ambiguous.

5. Evidentiary Issues

a. Lawrence J. Baer, Stacey L. Davidson, and Deborah S. K. Jagoda, essay, *Discovering Sexual Relations–Balancing the Fundamental Right to Privacy Against the Need for Discovery in a Sexual Harassment Case*, 25 NEW ENG. L. REV. 849 (Spring, 1991).

Short piece that merely points to the difficulty in balancing third-party privacy rights against the need for discovery. Author notes that in sexual harassment cases discovery disputes will continue until the courts come up with a working doctrine that takes both of these interests into account.

b. Linda J. Krieger and Cindi Fox, article, *Evidentiary Issues in Sexual Harassment Litigation*, 1 BERKELEY WOMEN'S L. J. 115 (Fall, 1985).

Though not the most current, this article remains timely since evidentiary issues regarding the admissibility of past sexual behavior and provocative dress evidence is hotly disputed. Concludes that victim's past sexual history is not admissible under any theory of evidence absent special circumstances. Evidence of harasser's past conduct, however, is relevant to establishing essential elements of the claim and is therefore admissible.

6. Employer Liability

a. Richard Luke Gemma, case note, *An Equitable Liability Standard for Offensive Work Environment Claims Under Title VII: Meritor Savings Bank v. Vinson*, 29 B. C. L. REV. 509 (March, 1988).

Superficial analysis of the Supreme Court's decision in *Meritor*. Author feels that the balance struck in *Meritor* is equitable because it protects employees' interests by providing legal redress for harassment, yet protects employers from liability without notice.

b. Kathleen A. Smith, note, *Employer Liability for Sexual Harassment: Inconsistency Under Title VII*, 37 Cath. Y. L. Rev. 245 (Fall, 1987).

Compares differing standards of employer liability under quid pro quo and hostile environment sexual harassment claims. Suggests that a uniform standard should be adopted. Also includes an enlightening comparison of the different treatment given Title VII claims based on sex, and Title VII claims based on race, religion, and national origin.

c. Ronald Turner, article, *Employer Liability Under Title VII for Hostile Environment Sexual Harassment by Supervisory Personnel: The Impact and Aftermath of Meritor Savings Bank*, 33 How. L. J. 1 (1990).

Outstanding article on the subject of employer liability. Article analyzes the Supreme Court's holding in *Meritor*, as well as the EEOC Guidelines, and lower-court decisions following *Meritor*. After a thorough analysis of the law, author concludes that in the absence of a definitive ruling on employer liability in *Meritor*, the lower courts have continued to apply agency principles in a way that holds employers directly liable for harassment by supervisory personnel.

d. Katherine S. Anderson, note, *Employer Liability Under Title VII for Sexual Harassment After Meritor Savings Bank v. Vinson*, 87 Colum. L. Rev. 1258 (October, 1987).

Analysis applies to harassment of women by women, as well as to harassment of women by men. Surveys other circuits to see how the issue of employer liability has been treated and analyzes the position of the EEOC and the Supreme Court. Concludes that employers should be vicariously liable for harassment by supervisors and should be liable only upon notice of harassment by co-workers.

e. Martha Sperry, comment, *Hostile Environment Sexual Harassment and the Imposition of Liability Without Notice: A Progressive Approach to Traditional Gender Roles and Power Based Relationships*, 24 New Eng. L. Rev. 917 (Spring, 1990).

Discusses the application of agency principles to employer liability for acts of supervisory employees which create a hostile working environment. Surveys the court decisions and finds that state courts are somewhat more willing to hold employers vicariously liable in these circumstances without a notice requirement. Federal courts, on the other hand, follow EEOC recommendations that actual or constructive notice is required for a finding of liability.

f. Lucy B. Longstreth, case, *Hostile Environment Sexual Harassment: A Wrong Without a Remedy?–Meritor Savings Bank v. Vinson, 106 S. Ct. 2399 (1986)*, 21 SUFFOLK U. L. REV. 811 (Fall, 1987).

Very short piece in which author explains that employers should be held strictly liable for the acts of their supervisory personnel that violate Title VII by creating a hostile working environment. She rejects the distinction between the quid pro quo standard and hostile environment standard as artificial.

g. Lisa A. Blanchard, note, *Sexual Harassment in the Workplace: Employer Liability for a Sexually Hostile Environment*, 66 WASH. U. L. Q. 91 (Winter, 1988).

Note considers different standards for employer liability under the EEOC Guidelines, federal law, and traditional agency principles, Recognizes the absence of a definite standard and proposes strategies to aid employers in avoiding liability in this uncertain field. Suggestions include adoption of a stringent anti-harassment policy, an effective grievance procedure, and active enforcement of the plan.

h. Colleen M. Davenport, case note, *Sexual Harassment Under Title VII: Equality in the Workplace or Second-Class Status?: Meritor Savings Bank, FSB v. Vinson, 106 S. Ct. 2399 (1986)*, 10 HAMLINE L. REV. 193 (February, 1987).

Although not exclusively on the hostile environment claim, this comment is valuable for its close analysis of Title VII's language. Author argues that employers should be held strictly liable for the sexual misconduct of their supervisors since both Title VII and the EEOC Guidelines do not require employer knowledge for liability.

i. Anne Clevy, article, *The Change in Employer Liability for Supervisor Sexual Harassment After Meritor: Much Ado about Nothing,* 42 ARK. L. REV. 795 (Fall, 1989).

Good summarization of agency principles and application of these principles to hostile environment cases. Proper application of agency principles, states author, will result in a finding of strict liability for supervisors. Suggests that courts have come to conflicting results since *Meritor* due to their inability to reconcile *Meritor's* mixed messages regarding employer liability.

j. Bruce Chandler Smith, comment, *When Should an Employer Be Held Liable for the Sexual Harassment by a Supervisor Who Creates a Hostile Work Environment? A Proposed Theory of Liability,* 19 ARIZ. ST. L. J. 285 (1987).

Read for discussion of the nature and scope of sexual harassment in general and a review of the important cases. Also analyzes *Meritor* and addresses issue of the bifurcated employer liability standard. On the issue of employer liability, the author proposes that courts must adopt broader agency themes to effectuate the remedial purpose of Title VII.

7. Proposals for Change

a. Judith A. Winston, symposium, *Civil Rights Legislation in the 1990's: Mirror, Mirror on the Wall: Title VII, Section 1981, and the Intersection of Race and Gender in the Civil Rights Act of 1990,* 79 CALIF. L. REV. 775 (1991).

Article includes three case studies, one of which focuses on a racial/sexual harassment hostile environment claim under Title VII, *Brooms v. Regal Tube Co.,* 881 F.2d 412 (7th cir. 1989). Case study is used to illustrate the special need for sexual harassment legislation that would provide an adequate remedy for women of color.

b. Cathleen Marie Mogan, note, *Current Hostile Environment Sexual Harassment Law: Time to Stop Defendants From Having Their Cake and Eating it Too*, 6 NOTRE DAME J. L. ETHICS & PUB. POL'Y 543 (1992).

According to the author, Title VII does not adequately address the problem of sexual harassment at work. While she recognizes that a federal statute that allows for private claims would be a quick solution to the problem, she also suggests the interim alternative of lowering the burden of proof standards under Title VII when plaintiffs are seeking only equitable remedies.

c. Theodore F. Claypoole, comment, *Inadequacies in Civil Rights Law: The Need for Sexual Harassment Legislation*, 48 OHIO ST. L. J. 1151 (Fall, 1987).

In advocating adoption of sexual harassment legislation, this comment outlines the remedies available under a hostile environment claim. Author proposes legislative adoption of the quid pro quo and hostile environment claims currently recognized, but with assignment of liability to both the harassing employee and his or her employer.

d. Ellen Frankel Paul, article, *Sexual Harassment as Sex Discrimination: A Defective Paradigm*, 8 YALE L. & POL'Y. REV. 333 (1990).

Author suggests that a new sexual harassment tort scheme would better address the issue of sexual harassment than does Title VII's discrimination framework. Explains the problems with characterizing sexual harassment as discrimination, then proposes her alternative.

e. Michelle Ridgeway Peirce, note, *Sexual Harassment and Title VII–A Better Solution*, 30 B. C. L. REV. 1071 (July, 1989).

Author notes that Title VII fails to address bisexual harassment as well as harassment in a single-sex environment. In response to this observation, she proposes legislation that would compensate victims of harassment based on gender and on sexuality. Suggests that such legislation would encourage courts to face gender issues rather than focus on physical harassment.

f. Michael O. Vhay, comment, *The Harms of Asking: Towards a Comprehensive Treatment of Sexual Harassment*, 55 U. CHI. L. REV. 328 (Winter, 1988).

   While this comment does not focus on the hostile environment claim alone, it does trace the history of the claim. Also proposes a new tort called "advances in inappropriate contexts," which would provide a better remedy for harassment victims than Title VII.

g. Susan M. Matthews, article, *Title VII and Sexual Harassment: Beyond Damages Control,* 3 YALE J. L. & FEMINISM 299 (Spring, 1991).

   Author states that Congress has failed to address some substantial obstacles that victims of sexual harassment continue to face. In particular, she cites inappropriate standards of proof and admission of victim's sexual history as obstacles that unfairly burden sexual harassment plaintiffs.

8. Other

a. Sally E. Barker and Loretta K. Haggard, article, *A Labor Union's Duties and Potential Liabilities Arising Out of Co-worker Complaints of Sexual Harassment,* 11 ST. LOUIS U. PUB. L. REV. 135 (Spring, 1992).

   Authors look at problem of conflicting duties that unions have to complainants and perpetrators in co-worker sexual harassment cases. They suggest policies for unions to follow in order to deal fairly and effectively with such situations.

b. Nicolé D. Rizzolo, comment, *A Right With Questionable Bite: The Future of "Abusive or Hostile Work Environment" Sexual Harassment as a Cause of Action for Women in a Gender-Based Society and Legal System,* 23 NEW ENG. L. REV. 263 (Summer, 1988).

Identifies prejudicial treatment of female litigators, litigants, and witnesses in the legal system as a major obstacle to women bringing hostile environment claims. This prejudice affects hostile environment claims more so than other claims because credibility is so crucial to recovery. Author lists suggestions which she feels would alleviate the problem, but does not explain them in any depth.

c. Amy Horton, comment, *Of Supervision, Center Folds, and Censorship: Sexual Harassment, the First Amendment, and the Contents of Title VII*, 46 U. MIAMI L. REV. 403 (November, 1991).

Thorough and well-written analysis of issue that will prove to be the upcoming battleground in sexual harassment cases. Article uses *Robinson v. Jacksonville Shipyards, Inc.* as a touchstone for discussion of this constitutional defense to workplace harassment. Part V focuses primarily on pin-ups.

d. Marcy Strauss, article, *Sexist Speech in the Workplace*, 25 HARV. CIV. RIGHTS. CIV. LIB. L. REV. 1 (Winter, 1990).

Important to see since free speech and the First Amendment promises to be a highly contested issue in sexual harassment law in the years to come.

e. Susan A. Fitzgibbon, speech, *Sexual Harassment and Labor Arbitration*, 20 GA. J. INT'L & COMP L. 71 (1990).

Asks whether arbitration offers any advantages over court trials in the resolution of sexual harassment claims. Examines the pros and cons of arbitration and concludes by explaining the reasons why victims should prefer arbitration.

f. Fran Sepler, article, *Sexual Harassment: From Protective Response to Proactive Prevention*, 11 HAMLINE J. PUB. L. & POL'Y 61 (Spring, 1990).

Discusses the need to define what sexual harassment is– what it looks like. Asks how to determine what constitutes a pattern of harassing behavior, focusing on the need for prevention techniques.

g. Wendy Pollack, article, *Sexual Harassment: Women's Experience vs. Legal Definitions*, 13 HARV. WOMEN'S L. J. 35 (Spring, 1990).

Criticizes the courts for legitimizing harassment through legal concepts that celebrate autonomy, privacy, and neutrality, all to the detriment of women. Focuses on the hostile environment claim.

h. Susan M. Faccenda, note, *The Emerging Law of Sexual Harassment: Relief Available to the Public Employee*, 62 NOTRE DAME L. REV. 677 (1987).

Recognizes the hostile environment claim as one option for a public employee who is the victim of sexual harassment. Outlines the history and requirements of the claim. Looks at other state and federal laws that allow recovery for harassment and argues that the remedies offered by Title VII are inadequate.

i. Eleanor K. Bratton, article, *The Eye of the Beholder: An Interdisciplinary Examination of Law and Social Research on Sexual Harassment*, 17 N. M. L. REV. 91 (Winter, 1987).

Author points to the interdependence of the legal and social science disciplines in the area of sexual harassment. Existing definitions of sexual harassment are rejected, but author makes no suggestion for a replacement. Instead, encourages that more thought, free from gender bias, be devoted to this issue.

j. Holly B. Fechner, note, *Toward an Expanded Conception of Law Reform: Sexual Harassment Law and the Reconstruction of Facts*, 23 U. MICH. J. L. REF. 475 (Spring, 1990).

Author notes that reformers have concentrated on changing legal doctrine, but have neglected to recognize that facts are just as important to the court decisions. She argues that reformers should focus on facts, because the reconstruction of factual descriptions will lead to a change in the law. This dynamic is illustrated through a case study of *Rabidue v. Osceola Refining Co.*, 805 F.2d 611 (6th Cir. 1986).

k. Barbara A. Gutek, article, *Understanding Sexual Harassment at Work*, 6 NOTRE DAME J. L. ETHICS & PUB. POL'Y 335 (1992).

Not on the hostile environment claim specifically, but on facts versus misconceptions about human behavior in the field of sexual harassment. Facts about the frequency and impact of sexual behavior at work are discussed as well as sex role spillover into the workplace environment.

I. LEGAL ENCYCLOPEDIAS

For someone who knows nothing about this area of law, encyclopedias are a good place to start. Encyclopedias provide a clear and concise description of the hostile environment claim and give you a feel for sexual harassment law in general. Such an understanding is necessary before getting lost in judicial opinions and journal articles. Between *American Jurisprudence 2nd* and *Corpus Juris Secundum*, only the former is worth seeing.

45 Am. Jur. 2d *Job Discrimination* §781 lists and briefly describes the elements of the hostile environment claim. Am. Jur. also illustrates fact patterns that constitute prohibited hostile environments and makes recommendations for employers to avoid liability. To find entries on point look up "Job Discrimination - Sexual Harassment" in Am. Jur.'s General Index. See §778-§816 for coverage of such topics as public employees' harassment claims, uninvolved employees, constructive discharge, effect of state fair employment laws, burdens of proof. Employers should also see the checklist of employer actions to avoid liability (§815) and the suggested employer policy statement (§816).

J. LEGISLATIVE HISTORY

Since sex was added as a protected category to Title VII of the Civil Rights Act of 1964 in a last-ditch attempt to defeat its passage, legislative history is not a rich resource of information on the hostile environment claim. To locate the history of Title VII's amendments or proposed amendments, researchers should try CCH's *Con-*

gressional Index, CIS/Index, Congressional Record, or *U.S. Code Congressional and Administrative News.*[5] These finding tools will lead you to enlightening debates, committee reports, and hearings on issues related to hostile environment sexual harassment.

K. NEWSPAPER AND MAGAZINE ARTICLES

There have been too many news and magazine articles written on sexual harassment to make recommendations on which ones to read. Usually popular articles either discuss the problem of sexual harassment in a very general way or report on pending legal claims. While such articles do not offer much in the way of substantive legal knowledge, they do furnish valuable supplemental information. Despite the difficulty of accessing popular articles, they should not be overlooked. Legal newspapers are more likely to discuss substantive legal issues, but do not provide the depth of law review articles.

Since the 1991 confirmation hearings of Clarence Thomas, there has been a surge of attention given to sexual harassment issues in the media. If you are interested in locating popular or legal articles, see Part III for more information. The articles that follow are included only to illustrate the type of information relevant to the hostile environment claim that is available in periodicals.

1. Popular Periodicals

Sex and Power in the Office, THE WALL ST. J., Oct. 18, 1991 at B1.

The entire Marketplace section is devoted to the topic of sexual harassment in employment. Presents a picture of where the public stands on the issue of sexual harassment today. Section includes such articles as, *Are You from Another Planet or What?, The Fall of Sister Power, Is That Supposed to Be Funny? Office Humor Is Facing New Test, Attractiveness Aids Men More Than Women, Romancing Co-Workers Gets Riskier, "Unwanted Advances" Affect Men, Too. Ask Gary Showalter, In Many Small Businesses Harassment Is Big Worry,*

Men Fight Back as Accusations Increase, Pursuing Complaint to the End Almost Ruins One Victim's Life, Women Lost Ground in 1980's and EEOC Didn't Help, and *Is a Dream Workplace Any Closer to Reality?*

2. Legal Periodicals

a. Cook, *The New Bias Battleground: Sex Harassment; Ruling to Spur Suits,* NAT'L L. J., July 7, 1986 at 1.

Author analyzes *Meritor* from the standpoint of its potential to increase sexual harassment cases brought into the court system. Includes valuable statistics as well as statements from representatives of the EEOC, Women's Legal Defense Fund, and others on this subject.

b. McCandless and Sullivan, *Two Courts Adopt New Standard to Determine Sexual Harassment,* NAT'L L. J., May 6, 1991 at 18.

Authors review *Ellison v. Brady,* 924 F.2d 872 (9th Cir. 1990), and *Robinson v. Jacksonville Shipyards, Inc.* 760 F. Supp. 1486 (M.D. Fla. 1991), two recent court decisions that have employed the reasonable woman standard in determining whether sexual harassment was sufficiently pervasive so as to create a hostile working environment.

c. Simonoff and Wallach, *Courts Draw the Liability Line on Work Place Sex Harassment,* NAT'L L. J., Feb. 13, 1989 at 21.

Great analysis of the Supreme Court's holding on employer liability in *Meritor.* Authors review each circuit's stance on the varying requirements for employer liability under a hostile environment claim for co-worker and supervisor harassment. Also includes suggestions for effective policies.

L. PRACTITIONER TOOLS

Listed below are publications that attorneys who represent victims of hostile environment sexual harassment will find useful. All three are particularly good and include collateral reference services that offer citations to all sorts of valuable information on the legal claim.

1. *Sex Discrimination: Sexual Harassment. Creating a Hostile Work Environment*, 50 Am. Jur. P.O.F. 2nd 127 (Lawyers Co-op. Pub. Co., 1988).

The best tool a lawyer could ask for. Addressed specifically to the issue of proving facts in a hostile environment sexual harassment case. Provides a step-by-step guide for attorneys bringing such a claim. Author looks separately at the testimony of the plaintiff, examination of the harasser, and the testimony of employees with knowledge of the acts. Updated with paper supplement which provides references to collateral resources on the hostile environment claim.

2. *Job Discrimination*, 21 Fed. Proc. L. Ed. 51 (1984).

Another invaluable practitioner tool. Chapter 50 discusses administrative and judicial procedural requirements to redress claims under Title VII. Covers filing complaint with local, state, or federal agency, investigations, conciliation efforts, right to sue letters, prerequisites to bring suits, standing, pleading, and proving discrimination, and available relief.

3. *Job Discrimination*, 12 Fed. Proc. Forms. L. Ed. 1. (1989).

Chapter 45 contains forms and procedural guides relating to administrative and judicial proceedings under Title VII. Reproduces EEOC forms and explains how they should be completed. Updated by pocket part. Also cites other practice aids.

M. STATISTICAL SURVEYS

The first publicized surveys on sexual harassment in the workplace conducted in the 1970s helped focus courts' attention on the need to establish a legal framework that prohibited such behavior.

Survey results in this field now provide information necessary to assess the success or failure of the legal framework established. Unfortunately, many results demonstrate widespread incidences of sexual harassment in employment. Such information may be pertinent, depending on your research goals. Popular periodicals usually cover the results of major surveys. For an evaluation of the various periodical indexes, see Part III. Some of the most publicized surveys include the following:

1. Nancy Dodd McCann and Thomas A. McGinn, *Harassed: 100 Women Define Inappropriate Behavior in the Workplace* (Business One Irwin, 1992).

2. Couric, *Women in the Large Firms: A High Price of Admission?* NAT'L L. J. December 11, 1989 at S2.

3. Sandorff, *Sexual Harassment in the Fortune 500*, WORKING WOMAN, December, 1988 at 69.

4. CRULL, THE IMPACT OF SEXUAL HARASSMENT ON THE JOB: A PROFILE OF THE EXPERIENCES OF 92 WOMEN (Working Women's Institute, Research Series Report No. 2, 1978).

5. U. S. Merit Systems Protection Board, Sexual Harassment in the Federal Workplace; An Update (U.S. Government Printing Office, 1988).

6. Safran, *What Men Do to Women on the Job: A Shocking Look at Sexual Harassment*, REDBOOK, November, 1976 at 149.

N. TEXTBOOKS

For anyone interested in textbooks, these two provide the best coverage of the hostile environment claim.

1. LINDGRIN AND TAUB, THE LAW OF SEX DISCRIMINATION (West Pub. Co., 1988).

2. HILL, SEX-BASED DISCRIMINATION (West Pub. Co., 1988).

O. TREATISES

The treatises listed below are the most relevant to the hostile environment claim. While their explanations of the claim are quite limited, the treatises contain other information on administrative requirements, discovery, and other procedural matters that practitioners may find helpful.

1. ABERNATHY AND SCHULMAN, THE LAW OF EQUAL EMPLOYMENT OPPORTUNITY (Warren, Graham & Lamont, 1990).

    Current and well-organized coverage of the state of the law. For information on the hostile environment claim, see §5.06, Sexual Harassment and Sexual Favors.

2. LARSON AND LARSON, EMPLOYMENT DISCRIMINATION (Matthew Bender).

    Similar to *Sex-Based Employment Discrimination* described below, this treatise provides a summary of the law as well as references to full-text resources. Discrimination based on sex is covered in the first binder of this four-binder set. For information on sexual harassment see §41.60.

3. MODJESKA, EMPLOYMENT DISCRIMINATION LAW, 2nd Ed. (Lawyers Co-op. Pub. Co., 1988).

    Only short coverage of hostile environment claim (§1:36), but Chapter 2 covering procedural issues related to Title VII may be helpful.

4. OMILIAN AND KAMP, SEX-BASED EMPLOYMENT DISCRIMINATION (Callaghan & Company).

    This treatise offers an editorial summation of the law with references to full-text resources. Chapter 21: "Theory of Sexual Harassment Case," and Chapter 22: "Prima Facie Case Under Title VII," are the places to look for information relevant to the hostile environment claim.

5. RUZICHO, JACOBS AND THRASHER, EMPLOYMENT DISCRIMINATION LITIGATION (Anderson Pub. Co., 1989).

Offers great litigation advice tailored to employment discrimination cases. For information on the hostile environment claim in particular see §1.28, Harassment and Hostile Environment.

NOTES

1. See Part III for more information on conducting on-line research.
2. See Part III for information on finding a specialized library in your area.
3. 477 U.S. 57 (1986).
4. For EEOC regulations see 29 CFR §1604.11.
5. For most recent version write your local EEOC office or see BNA's Fair Empl. Proc. Manual [Lab. Rel. Rep.] 405:6681.

Index